Pierre Loti:
Romance of a Great Writer

As a boy, Loti felt the call of the unknown. 'I will wander all the world over,' he told himself, 'and return, a grey-haired man, to the home of my fathers to muse on the strange and beautiful things I have seen.' This ambition was realised. Entering the French Navy, Loti saw the world from shipboard. He spent long months among the palm groves of the South Seas; he visited the scorching coast of Senegal and the wild seas of Iceland. And every strange and exotic scene he made the background of a love story. In this life, written with fervent sympathy, we journey with Loti from Brittany to Constantinople, from China to Morocco, from Egypt to Ispahan, breathing all the way the atmosphere and recognising the sources of the stories which have delighted the peoples of all lands. Readers will find the biography of Pierre Loti as fascinating as the tales for which he is so deservedly renowned.

Edward B. D'Auvergne was a noted biographer.

T0348034

The Pierre Loti Library

Siam

Aziyadé

Egypt

Japan
Madame Chrysanthemum

Morocco

India

Japan and Corea

The Sahara to Senegal

Jerusalem and the Holy Land

Tahiti
The Marriage of Loti

The Iceland Fisherman

A Tale of the Pyrenees

A Tale of Brittany

Pierre Loti: Romance of A Great Writer
Edward B. D'Auvergne

PIERRE LOTI.

(After a painting by Lévy d'Hurmer.)

Pierre Loti:
Romance of a Great Writer

Edward B. D'Auvergne

Routledge
Taylor & Francis Group

LONDON AND NEW YORK

First published 2002 by Kegan Paul Limited

Distributed by:
Turpin Distribution & Columbia University Press

Published 2018 by Routledge
2 Park Square, Milton Park, Abingdon, Oxon OX14 4RN
52 Vanderbilt Avenue, New York, NY 10017

First issued in paperback 2018

*Routledge is an imprint of the Taylor & Francis Group, an informa
business*

British Library Cataloguing in Publication Data
A catalogue record for this book is available from the British Library.

Library of Congress Cataloging-in-Publication Data
Applied for.

ISBN 13: 978-1-138-98552-0 (pbk)
ISBN 13: 978-0-7103-0864-1 (hbk)

PREFACE

THIS is not a review of the literary activities of a great writer. Loti's place in the literature of France has been established by his contemporaries, and only a distant posterity can revise that verdict. I have been drawn to write the story of his life because I loved the man—loved him since a certain dark day long ago, when in a mood which he would so well have understood, I happened to read his *Aziyade*. The sympathy I felt for him then became warmer as I knew more about him—in spite of, or, I should say, because of the many weaknesses which a closer study of his character revealed. He would have forgiven me, I am sure, for saying that I think I understand him. And it seems to me that his life may enable others to understand him, and what he wrote, somewhat better.

EDMUND B. D'AUVERGNE

The Third Anniversary of Loti's death.

CONTENTS

CONTENTS

LIST OF ILLUSTRATIONS

PIERRE LOTI

The Romance of a Great Writer

CHAPTER I

THE FATHER TO THE MAN

ONE April evening, some sixty odd years ago, a boy sat at the window of a top room in the French sea-port town of Rochefort. His gaze took in the trees on the wall built by Louis Quatorze, and beyond, the silver thread of the river Charente. But his vision extended farther afield—beyond the near-by ocean, far ahead into the years. He beheld his future life unrolled before him as a gorgeous epic, played out with the whole world for a background. Farther and farther he peered into the unborn years till, a grey-headed man, he loomed up in this very room, to murmur with a sigh of resignation, "I have been everywhere, I have seen everything. I have done everything. . . . In the heart of the forests of Siam, I have seen the star of eve rise above the ruined temple of Angkor."

The boy was Julien Viaud. The man was Pierre Loti. And as the boy dreamed, so it all came to pass.

I

"I know not," says Loti, "whether many men in their childhood have thus seen their whole life in true prospect. But nothing has happened to me which I did not vaguely foresee from my earliest years."

The circumstances of his upbringing were decisive in shaping this essentially romantic conception of himself. At least, I know cases where the like environment has produced an exactly similar attitude in people of very different ancestry. Pierre Loti was the Benjamin of his family, born to his parents in their middle age, seeming, as he tells us, to belong in his own home to another generation. He was born at Rochefort on January 14, 1850. Louis Marie Julien were the names given him in baptism. His father, Jean Theodore, was a native of Rochefort who had married Nadine Texier, a staunch Huguenot, and embraced her religion with fervour. The Texiers had suffered for their faith in times past, probably they had been among the defenders of La Rochelle. The dour features of the French Protestants, as of the Scottish Covenanters, have been glorified and softened in the eyes of posterity by the martyr's halo, and Louis Julien, though he soon lost their faith, never ceased to venerate the memory of his mother's ancestors. Indeed, he seems everywhere in his works to set much more store by them than by his father's, though his paternal grandfather had died of wounds received at Trafalgar, and another Viaud had left behind him a book which proves him to have been an intrepid and widely-travelled navigator.*

* A fact elucidated by M. Serban in his authoritative life of Loti.

2

At the time of his birth, Loti's father was forty-six years old, his mother forty. They already had a daughter, Marie, then in her nineteenth year, and another son, Gustave, aged twelve. The baby thus found himself surrounded not only by seniors, but by quite old people, with whom the little house in the Rue St. Pierre, since so much enlarged and aggrandised, was crowded. There were grandmothers and aunts, all of them a good deal surprised, no doubt, by the infant's arrival.

The Viauds were not rich. The father held the important but not very profitable office of Secretary to the Commune, or, in other words, Town Clerk. They led a dull, prim life, and no doubt considered it incumbent upon them, as adherents of "the religion," to set a good example to their Catholic neighbours. The children were brought up, as we should think, strictly. They assisted at the grim services at the Temple. Little Julien, we are informed, was heard to grumble: "Always getting up, always going to bed, always nasty soup!" It was, in fact, the kind of home which English novelists are never tired of picturing and girding at. How often is our sympathy invoked for the lonely, dreamy child, fettered by harsh conventions, stifling in the mean, narrow world of Protestantism, always misunderstood by his parents and, indeed, by everybody except some childless uncle or aunt! We breathe a sigh of relief when the child, grown into the hero or heroine, leaves the paternal roof, to find a spiritual home in furnished rooms off King's Road, S.W.3, or in Gt. James Street, W.C.1. We can, therefore, better imagine this emancipated young person's amazement upon reading the French author's recollections of his childhood and his father's house.

These memories were, in fact, his tenderest and fondest. With loving detail, he reproduces the atmosphere of his birthplace, the lineaments of his first friends. Rochefort itself does not impress the stranger as an interesting place. It was founded as a naval station by Louis XIV's minister, Colbert, and not a house within its seventeenth century ramparts can be more than three hundred years old. The country round about—which once belonged to the old province of Saintonge—is flat, tame, and cut up like a chess board by the indefatigable French *cultivateur*. Loti knew that his native land was far from beautiful; he refers more than once to "the poor plains of my Saintonge"; but to the last day of his life he loved the place, not merely because it was the spot where the romance of his life began, but because it was hallowed by the memory of his parents and kinsfolk.

Of his father, oddly enough, I can find no picture. His earliest recollection of his mother is, on the contrary, distinct and durable. She was then, he calculates, about forty-six, but in comparison with other members of the household, she might well have seemed, even to childish eyes, quite young. But "I was without the faintest idea as to my mother's age," he tells us, "I never asked myself whether she was young or old. It was only later that I noticed even she was distinctly pretty." His recollection of her he communicates as follows:

LOTI AS A BOY OF FOUR.
(After an oil-painting by Madame Bon, sister of Pierre Loti.)

"I see her still, as she appeared at the door, bringing with her the sunshine and fresh air of outdoors. I remember everything—her expression as she looked at me, the sound of her voice, even the details of her dear dress which would seem so odd and antiquated to-day. She wore a straw hat with yellow roses and a shawl of lilac barège (shawls were in fashion then), flowered with little bunches of dark violet. Her black ringlets—those poor dear ringlets which have not changed their form*, but which are, alas! thinner and all white to-day—contained not a single strand of silver."

His brother, Gustave, following the family tradition, entered the Navy as a surgeon. He became in after years an heroic figure in Loti's memory, and to him he owed his vocation. He recalls his departure for his first cruise, but complains: "Perhaps I hadn't had time enough to know him, to attach myself to him, for he had early adopted a young man's life, thus separating himself a little from the rest of us. I seldom went into his room—the number of big books scattered about, the odour of cigars, and the likelihood of meeting his friends, officers and students, frightened me. I had been told, moreover, that he was not very good, that he used to go out in the evenings. They used to read him lectures, and, inwardly, I disapproved his conduct.

"But his approaching departure redoubled my affection and caused me a real sadness. He was going to Tahiti, in Polynesia, just at the end of the

* Written in 1889, seven years before the death of Mme. Viaud.

world, and his cruise would last four years, very nearly half the duration of my own life. . . . And the prospect of seeing him again was sadly spoiled by my being told that I should then be a big boy of twelve or thirteen." For he did not want to grow up. "I am afraid that I shall be miserable when I am big," he confessed. Like many other of our author's emotions and experiences, this dread was not so unusual as he fancied.

Upon the big brother's departure, the little one became more than ever the darling of the household. He admits, you see, that he had identified himself with the ideas of the elderly people, to whom he was now entirely abandoned. Of two or three of these kind people he has left us vivid pictures. There was his father's mother, widow of the man who had fallen at Trafalgar, who, now in her dotage, was for ever singing the *Marseillaise*, the *Chant du Départ*, the *Parisienne*, and other patriotic and martial airs of the heroic age to which she had belonged. With amusement, her grandson admits, not unmixed with bewilderment or without reverence, he used to see her bowing and chatting to her own reflection in the glass. But he was never frightened of her "because she continued quite definitely pretty . . ." and pretty she remained, when, within a very few years, the tiny boy saw her lying with her hands crossed on her bed and realised that here was death.

Then there was Grand Tante Berthe, another old lady, who used to call him to look at the sunset; and another aunt, not quite so old we gather,

Tante Claire, "the person above all others who spoilt me most." It was from Tante Claire (his mother's sister) that little Julien heard about his Huguenot ancestors and other stories of the "isle"— the isle was Oléron just across the water, which had so long been the refuge of the Texier and other Protestant families. Three more aunts still lived there, at the little town of St. Pierre. When Julien was taken to see them (he says) "It was a delight, mingled with all manner of uncomprehended emotions. . . . The dominant impression produced by these persons, the Huguenot austerity of their manner, their way of living, their house, was that all belonged to a vanished epoch, to an earlier age."

Reading these reminiscences, I find myself wondering whether they do not express rather the adult's than the child's view of his environment. For if the boy Louis Julien was able to idealise the man he was to be, so Pierre Loti was eminently capable of idealising the boy he had been. Our young men fresh from Oxford would prefer, as I have said, to represent themselves as sad, lonely, and misunderstood children; but that, of course, is not the Frenchman's way. Little Viaud did find life extremely monotonous at times—of that there can be no doubt; but a unique figure in the household, and screened from all contact with the world, he found refuge in a realm of fancy, a fairyland of which he was the fairy prince.

He was spared for a long time that desolating knowledge of one's own unimportance that comes from association with boys of one's own age. His education was taken in hand by Aunt Claire, assisted at times by his mother and his sister. Later on, tutors from outside were called in. He did not like them, and he liked study as little. Judged by French educational standards, he was a lazy, indifferent pupil. The future writer of so many books did not care for reading. His own thoughts were good enough entertainment. He found a fresh interest in his "museum," beginning with a collection of tropical shells and plants which had been given him by a great uncle, a retired ship's surgeon. He added to this collection in a haphazard way. His tastes were never scientific. The objects in his "museum" stimulated his imagination. He wove fancies about them as smaller children do about their toys.

Also, he had his playmates. If any of them were boys, he has not troubled to mention them. But at nine years of age he was writing letters full of affection to a little girl, whom he speaks of as Lucette. (In our country, by the way, a boy who could write well-expressed letters at the age of nine would not be accounted a bad scholar). Among the few real events of his childish existence were his visits to Lucette's home at La Limoise, a property situated on the other side of the Charente, about three miles from Rochefort. Other little girls flit through his memories of this time—Antoinette, Véronique, Jeanne. Probably, he cared for none of them so well as for his cat, quaintly named *La Suprématie*, a singularly unprepossessing specimen of his graceful kind. Loti's most lovable trait, his fondness for animals, showed itself very early in the day.*

At La Limoise, the child was first introduced to nature—to woods, fields and running brooks. Now he dreamed of mountains, as children born inland, he imagines, dream of the sea. A letter from his sister then travelling in Switzerland, quickened his yearning. Happily, a distant kinsman just then renewed his relations with the family, and invited Louis Julien to visit him at his home, Bretenoux, a village in the department of the Lot, at the foot fo the Cêvennes. And there the future traveller of the world beheld his first mountain.

"I was to pass several summers at this village," he writes, "and became so far acclimatised as to learn to speak the *patois* of the villagers. So that the two homelands of my childhood are Saintonge and this countryside, both regions of the sun. Brittany, which so many people have assigned me for my country, I did not see till I was seventeen, nor did I care for it till much later."

Castelnau, the ruined *château-fort* which dominated the village of Bretenoux—La Limoise—the Ile d'Oléron—his *musée*— and his friendships with Lucette and Véronique, were all, we see now, much more potent influences in shaping the man than the positive education received from tutors.

But now to his dismay, his parents, realising that he would have to meet other boys sooner or later, entered him as a day-boy at the College of Rochefort. The school is now a *lycée* and bears Pierre Loti's

* It was inherited from, or shared by his mother.

name. He conferred no lustre upon it, and was thoroughly unhappy there. His comrades, no doubt, regarded him as a mollycoddle and a prig. He would have had a worse time at an English school, where, indeed, his peculiar conception of himself would almost certainly have been knocked out of him. But he belonged to a nation which is ever more tolerant of individuality than we are, and though he was exposed to ridicule by being escorted to and from school by a servant, he had no occasion to complain of actual persecution.

This may have been because he proved no rival to his classmates. Regularly, it is true, he carried off the prize for Latin, but he was without ambition and application. Knowing that at West Point Stonewall Jackson gave no promise of soldierly genius, that the Prince Imperial at Sandhurst took only the third place in French, we are not surprised to hear that Loti, afterwards an Academician, was rated very low in regard to French composition. The prize was carried off by a boy who, in after years, became a bailiff in a particularly humdrum manufacturing town. That our boy took a whole summer to get through *Télémaque* will cause no surprise to anyone.

The dreariness of these school years was broken by the Sundays and the Thursday half-holidays, and by the visits to La Limoise and Bretenoux. From the latter place, he was recalled one day by a telegram announcing the return of his brother. Gustave, a bronzed, bearded sailor, considered him with a paternal eye, and seems to have hinted to his parents that the boy's character wanted stiffening. But Loti had little opportunity to open his heart to him. Surgeon Viaud was recalled from leave and ordered to join his ship, which was under orders for the East.

"The farewells this time," we read, "were not so sad as before, because we believed that he would be absent only two years. In reality it was the last farewell. He was gone for ever, and his body was to repose at the bottom of the Bay of Bengal.

"When he was gone from our sight, my mother turned to me with a look which moved me profoundly. Then drawing me to her she said, in a tone of complete confidence, 'Thank God, we shall always keep you at any rate.'"

Louis Julien hung his head. Keep him? keep him for ever in this dull town! It was then he realised that he had always intended to go away, to go away much farther than his brother, to roam the whole wide world. Once he had talked of being a pastor like the grave gentleman with the Geneva bands, who preached at him eternally on Sundays; once he had vowed to become a missionary; now within his weeping mother's embrace, bewildered yet enlightened, he surveyed the room made so empty by his brother's departure, and perceived that his vague yearnings, his long, long dreams, could be realised only in his brother's calling. Yes, it must be the sea. . . .

He was not in the least the kind of boy one would expect to become a sailor; one cannot picture the boy Loti standing at the salute and waving the tricolour above his head. I don't suppose at that time he knew any more than I do the French equivalent for "hearts of oak"! He admits that even at the moment he saw his gate opened before him, the prospect of the Navy frightened him. But he had sense enough to see that his dreams were not going to come true all of themselves, and that he was not going to find the strange world within the ramparts of Rochefort. Already, a certain direction had been given to his fancy by his "museum" by his brother's letters, and by an old forgotten ship's log, discovered at La Limoise. That the charms of the Tahitian damsels, crudely portrayed in a book of travels given him by Gustave, nerved him to his decision, I take leave to doubt. But the mariner's life, though the details might be unpleasant, appeared to him essentially picturesque.

A craving for romance—to be himself a hero of romance—that, I count, was the directing power of Pierre Loti's life. He was a capable musician, he was clever with his pencil, already he had committed his fancies to writing in a diary—but it would have shocked him to think of himself as anything so commonplace as an author or a pianist. I can remember when boys of his temperament all said they wanted to be soldiers or sailors. They know too much about the mechanical existence of both, to want to be either, now.

Young Viaud was in no hurry to announce his choice of a career. Things were pleasanter for him, now, at the college. He had made friends of two of the bigger boys. They talked together about girls. Paul and André had real sweethearts. Louis Julien, not to be outdone, affected a passion for his playmate, Jeanne, for whom, in reality, he had a perfectly simple comrade-like affection. But he felt obscurely the stirrings of sex. He tells us of phantoms which haunted his sleep.

It was beyond the sound of the sea, among the ruins of Castelnau, that he acted upon his resolution. He wrote to his brother, announcing his desire to enter the Navy. The decision, which so many boys would have taken without hesitation and with delight, cost him a violent mental struggle. It was with a very real effort that he addressed the envelope to his brother at some Far Eastern station, and with set teeth that he posted it. The die was cast! We can imagine Louis Julien Viaud straightening his shoulders, and looking with a proud, fine smile at the hushed heaven which witnessed an act so momentous.

"For the first time, life and the world were opened wide before me. A new light shone upon my path: a sad, subdued light, perhaps, but which penetrated to the farthest horizon, nearing death and old age.

"I saw myself in uniform, pacing the hot quay-side of exotic towns. I saw myself returning home, after perilous voyages, with monstrous packages, full of wonderful things. . . ." And at this point he almost wept at the thought of not seeing mother and Aunt Berthe for so long, perhaps never again!

He was now, he tells us, in his fifteenth year. After all, the decision was momentous, not only for him, but for us. Had he chosen any other profession, Louis Julien Viaud would not have become Pierre Loti. Ashore, he would have lived the life romantic, or rather the life passionate, but would never have become sufficiently detached to write about it. He was not rich enough to make himself like Byron, a Childe Harold at his own expense. Authorship for its own sake did not, as we have seen, attract him. As a clerk or a provincial notary, he would not have cared, I fancy, to parade his emotions and experiences. His self-respect demanded a spacious stage and a well-painted backcloth. And these, as a sailor, he got.

LOTI AS A BOY OF TWELVE.

LOTI AS A MIDSHIPMAN.

CHAPTER II

GROWING UP

HIS definite choice of a career Loti regards as marking the end of his childhood. He had conscripted himself into the ranks of men. Henceforward his gaze must be turned towards the real world. That it held sorrows, rather more real than those he had imagined hitherto, he was not long in finding out.

As to his vocation, we gather that he left it to his brother to announce his decision to their parents. They disapproved it. The boy was content to wait. He was not unduly eager, I suspect, to leave his home and the old familiar faces. But the old familiar faces were leaving him. His playmate, Lucette, had grown up abruptly as girls do, was married out of hand, and carried off by her new husband to French Guiana. Then—a thing never expected by a younger brother—his sister, Marie, more than eighteen years older than he, also got married to Armand Bon, a young man of her own age, and left him alone in a house of old people.

On the occasion of this marriage, Louis Julien attempted to choke down his emotion with champagne.

Loti recalls this as one of the only three occasions that he was drunk in all his life. "The second time was at New York when I was a midshipman, at the banquet of a temperance society. The third, was at Constantinople, when I was presented to the Commander of the Faithful, in the fairylike Yildiz Kiosk. . . . A certain sweet champagne was too much for me, and great was my confusion when I found that a sort of haze had formed between me and the Red Sultan, who motioned me to a chair by his side!"

Two or three seasons passed. Very soon now, both Gustave and Lucette would be home again. Louis Julien, looking up at the ceiling of the classroom and wriggling at his desk, began to count the days. Then, one hot Sunday in April, the bad news came. Gustave was dead. He had died at sea (March 10th, 1865) and buried in the Bay of Bengal. Loti went out into the garden and over a grotto built for his amusement by the good big brother, vowed him an eternal cult.

Two months later, under her father's roof, Marie Bon gave birth to a daughter. Louis Julien had hardly recovered from his surprise at finding himself an uncle, when he was called to see his old comrade Lucette. He started at the sight of her. The deadly air of the infernal Colony, to which France still sends her convicts, had done its work. The young wife died the morning after her return to her native town.

The fifteen-year old boy was staggered by these successive blows. His brother, his old playmate—

16

he was never to see them again. Life, then, was as sad as he had thought. But mingled with grief, Loti confesses, was personal fear—the fear that haunted him all his life, the fear that to some is so incomprehensible, the fear of death.

Decidedly, the old, young life was changing. Reverses overtook Jean Theodore Viaud—the father, whom his son hardly troubles to commemorate, but who, behind the scenes, was putting up a stiff, stout fight for wife and child and aged kinsfolk. The ancestral house on the Isle was sold, the house at Rochefort was let in great part to strangers. The lad could ill support this series of misfortunes. Sorrow at close view lost much of its romance. And he had no religious faith to console him. That had died long ago; and the theories of Comte, of which he had learnt something at school, have not so far inspired a Job.

Having lost one son at sea, the Viauds might naturally have shrunk from trusting the other one upon it; but their financial embarrassments forced them to subdue this reluctance. We are never told what his father had proposed to make of Louis Julien. Whatever his design might have been, he now saw fit to abandon it. Louis Julien would have to earn his own living. His sister, Marie Bon, told him that he was free to begin his studies for entrance to the Naval School.

Without any enthusiasm he accepted his destiny, entered the Navy class at his college, and passed the qualifying examination. It had been settled that he was to spend a year studying in Paris before he entered the Naval School at Brest. The weight of the examination off his mind, the seventeen-year old lad hurried off to pay a farewell visit to his great-uncle and to his sister who lived near by. In this interval there happened to him that event in life, which in the opinion of some changes the child into the adult, which most of us may remember but never talk about.

Loti thus traces the portrait of the first woman who taught him the meaning of sex: "Eighteen or twenty, perhaps, this gypsy girl, a little older than I; deeply tanned, the colour of old Etruscan terra cotta, with an exquisitely fine skin. Her poor dress, perfectly clean, hung close to her young statue's breast; her thick black hair was stuck with gilt pins. In her ears she wore thick gold rings, and round her throat a kerchief of red silk. But fascinating beyond all were her eyes, profound as the night; behind which, perhaps, there was, in fact, nothing, but which seemed to hide all the mystical sensuality of the Indies. Such eyes I was to see again, in the silk-clad bayadères of Hindu temples. . . ."

The young student met the gypsy, selling brooms or what not, at the door of his sister's house at St. Porchaire.* Rudely dismissed by the servant, the vagabond directed a curious look at him and went her way. The lad, all on fire with an instinct he could hardly have understood, tracked her to the encampment of her people in a wood near by. Every afternoon for five or six days, he repeated

* He calls this place Fontbruant.

the visit. Not a word passed between them. Before her frank stare and curious smile, he lowered his gaze in confusion. Then at last, she followed him into the wood, their hands touched, and— "the great secret of love and life was taught me there in an opening in the rocks, like the porch of a Cyclopean temple. All round were harts' tongue and delicate ferns. We lay on the rarest, richest mosses. . . ."

That is how the supreme experience of adolescence appeared to Loti, writing at the age of sixty-eight or sixty-nine. To the lad himself, its picturesque value was probably less apparent. He had scruples, fears, remorse—that is admitted; he revolted, I suspect, against the blind, ungovernable force within him. But to the old man it was sweet and memorable, that initiation into the passion which was to procure him the most exquisite sensations of his life. Conscious of having painted the theatre of the episode a degree too vividly, he adds, "The places where we have neither loved nor suffered leave no impression on our memory. On the other hand, the spots where our senses were enraptured are never forgotten."

We have here* a vivid and curiously fresh revelation of an experience about which the overwhelming majority of men are silent. An Anglo-Saxon writer would have pretended that the rustic simplicity of the gypsy maid awakened a pure and chivalrous feeling in the young student—that it was Divine Nature, whispering in the woodland, which betrayed

* *Prime Jeunesse* Ch. XXVIII.

the two young things in their complete innocence . . . But love was never less beautiful in Loti's eyes because it was undistinguishable from lust. He tells us, indeed, that on finding his gypsy gone, at the thought of the tenderness in her eyes, he shed tears; but the tenderness, perhaps, existed rather in the imagination of age than in the passionate recollection of the boy.

The girl had gone out of his sight and ken for ever. In the anguish of leaving home and kindred, he forgot all about her, as, in the time to come, he was to forget so many light o' loves. In October, 1866, he went to Paris to continue his studies at the Lycée Henri-Quatre.

For him, the capital of Napoleon III and Eugénie, brighter and richer than it has ever been before or since, was simply a place of exile. Louis Julien Viaud had no thought at that moment of earning a living with his pen. Otherwise he might have thought fit to affect the rapture so usual to the artistic or literary young man upon arriving in London or Paris. He did not sit up at his window all night, gazing out upon the city which he proposed to conquer; instead, I rather think he laid his face upon his hands and wept bitterly. From the window of his lodging overlooking St. Etienne du Mont, he saw only "a stupefying assembly of chimney-pots. It was sad enough to make one weep. . . ." The bats who flitted about, he held in kind remembrance. His thoughts, his heart, were back at Rochefort. He suffered (as Frenchmen do) agonies of home sickness. He wouldn't, he couldn't, see anything to admire in Paris. He refused even to be astonished. These first bitter impressions seem permanently to have clouded Loti's judgment. If he ever wrote a word in praise of the city, it has eluded me.

Loti is rather inclined to stress his native delicacy and the refinement of his manners, and to complain of the vulgarity of the Latin Quarter; but it is likely enough that to his companions he appeared a raw, homespun youth. He made an effort, at least, to fall into their ways.

"I hung about," he confesses, "the usual resorts of the *Rive Gauche ;* but my manner was variable, abrupt and awkward, scared, like a bird put full-grown in a cage. I had a good many surprises. The only memories I have carried away were of dull, sickening, unhealthy things. People have sung that sort of life. Personally, I am without taste for the poetry of the garret, the grisette, and the estaminet."*

The instinct first obeyed in the woods of Font-bruant led him, however, into fugitive liaisons in the great city. He finds it hard to sentimentalise about these, and obviously prefers the half-savage charms of the gypsy to the coquetterie of the grisette. All the while, he was eating his heart out. He covered pages of his diary with reminiscences of Rochefort, the Isle, and La Limoise—writings which were no unworthy prelude to his life's work.

At last, in July, 1867, came release. Louis Julien Viaud sat for the final examination for admission

* *Fleurs d'ennui.*

21

to the Naval School, and promptly said good-bye
to Paris. "I who have so often felt a pang in
leaving some merely temporary abode in different
parts of the world, I don't believe it occurred to me
to bestow a single backward glance at the room
where I had studied and had passed the long winter
hours, looking across at the spire of St. Etienne du
Mont." A few hours later and he was home again,
in the arms of his adored and adoring family.
Between him and his cat, *La Suprématie*, there was
a specially touching reunion.

He knew that he had qualified. In the delight of
finding himself again among the dear familiar faces
and places, he may possibly have wished that he
had failed. For the next separation would be a long
one, his definite abandonment of his father's roof-
tree. But there was no going back now. He
admits he could never have reconciled himself to
a desk in some *administration* like his father's. And
the poverty to which his family had now grown
pretty well accustomed, made it absolutely necessary for him to earn his living as early as possible.

He begrudged, he tells us, every hour he was
forced to spend away from Rochefort. But he had
to pay a visit to his sister at Saint Porchaire, and
it was there, by his brother-in-law, that he was
shown the *Moniteur* (the official Gazette) announcing
that he had passed. After a glimpse, as we are free to
suppose, at the scene of his first amour, he returned
to Rochefort. A few days after, and Theodore and
Nadine Viaud saw their only surviving son quit

their house to follow the sea, which had taken his brother to its depths.

Loti entered the Imperial Navy on October 1, 1867—the date he was received as a cadet on the training ship *Borda,* stationed off Brest. He had accepted the calling with a singular lack of enthusiasm. Ships had never interested him; he had never even wished for a toy boat. This indifference, common enough in the commercial or clerical apprentice, is sufficiently rare in the naval cadet. Probably neither he nor his parents expected him to distinguish himself as a sailor. Yet he was to leave the Navy a rich and famous man, largely thanks to the influence of the sea, though by the exercise of a talent at that time quite unsuspected in him.

CHAPTER III

THE CADET.　FIRST OCEAN VOYAGES.　WAR

I HAVE never been to Brest, but from the position on
the map, I judge it to be as dismal a spot as any even
in Scotland and Ireland.　Nor do I know anything
about life on a training ship; but the combination
"life on a training ship off Brest" sounds to me
positively terrifying.　That poor little Viaud first
found it so I have no doubt at all, though writing
while he was a sailor of when he was a sailor, he is
careful not to say this precisely.

He does admit that the Breton town perched on
its high granite cliffs impressed him as lugubrious.
At that moment it may be that he preferred even
the view of St. Etienne du Mont.　When he clam-
bered aboard and found himself between decks, he
did not, let us hope, repeat the legend which Dante
read above the gates of Hell.

For all this unwonted reserve, the picture he
draws of life aboard the *Borda* is not cheerful.　"In
the floating cloister wherein our youth was abruptly
enclosed, life was rude and austere.　In several
respects, it was like that of the sailors.　Like them,
we lived much in the wind, in the fog, in the mist

which left on one's lips a taste of salt. Like them, we climbed the yards to furl sails, which tore our hands; we worked the guns with the old-fashioned tackle and tarred ropes; and in all weathers, generally blown about by the Western gales, we went for boat practice on the vast roadstead.

"During the hours of study, in the interior of the cloister, seated at our desks in the great gun rooms, we became absorbed in mathematics and astronomy. These studies were, in a way, soothing. They had a calming effect on our senses and imagination like muscular fatigue.

"Around us, under the clouded sky, the shifting haze of Brittany, presented a ceaseless phantasmagoria, transfiguring the granite coast and the eternal movement of the ocean.

"We who entered that autumn upon this monastic life were all between seventeen and eighteen years of age. Very dissimilar in tastes, education, and ideas, we fell, instinctively, from the first, into little groups, which endured to the end of our two years' novitiate. We never used the intimate 'thou' in addressing each other. A convention of courtesy ruled us to such a point that I have no recollection of any teasing or quarrels."

An atmosphere certainly different from that of *Mr. Midshipman Easy* or *Tom Cringle's Log*, but occasionally to be perceived around certain English messes. One is reminded, as perhaps the writer wished we should be, of French military life as described by de Vigny. Loti chose the most loosely organised of these groups, esteeming, as he wrote in the diary which he was required to keep at this time, that "individual liberty is one of the indispensable conditions of life."

Twice a week these well-behaved young sailors were marched through the streets of Brest and put through their infantry drill. Marching to the sound of fife and drum, his musket on his shoulder and bayonet at his side, should have refreshed Loti's romantic soul. On one of these occasions he remembers seeing "the professional beauty of Brest," and returned to his ship filled with thoughts of her. Even so young as this, he must have rebelled against his celibate life, and regretfully evoked the images of the gypsy lass and the grisettes of the Quartier. But we are told of no amours at this period, though excursions ashore, two or three times a week, might have provided the opportunity.

A shipmate writing in after years* recalls Loti as a reserved, sensitive youth, who did not at first make himself popular among the "midships." But he very much improved on closer acquaintance and responded readily to friendly advances. As he grew older, his good points were better appreciated, and he was well liked in the wardroom. The French youth is not as intolerant as the English of singularity or strong personality, but, in any case, Loti's extraordinary modesty must have prepossessed his fellows. When his literary fame had been noised all through France, he never troubled to proclaim his identity with the rising author. At last the secret came out. "Is it true that you are Pierre

---

* In the *Figaro* about the time of Loti's election to the Academy.

Loti?" asked a stupefied comrade who had been reading one of his works. "Yes," replied the young naval officer, meekly.

M. Serban, as a good biographer should, rather throws the blame on his hero's associates. "In the French Navy," he observes, "even to-day, and then more than now, an officer of modest origin always found himself left very much in the cold. For Loti, the situation was worse on account of his religion. Moreover, his very slender resources handicapped him seriously at the beginning of his career. But it is only by the title of the book covering his early life in the service—*A Poor Young Officer*—that he allows us to infer the bitterness his restricted means occasioned him." Certainly I find little in the body of the work to make us suppose that he was really unhappy as a cadet. None of the French naval officers I have met ever appeared to have any money or to expect other people to have any.

Light from another source has been thrown on Loti at this stage of his apprenticeship. Every year, the "*Bordassiens*" went for a cruise along the west coast of France in the corvette *Bougainville*. The log or journal of these voyages, which every cadet was required to keep, is Loti's first book of travel. It was found and made the subject of a careful analysis by M. Michael Salomon.* The extracts undoubtedly evince the author's native literary sense. The Bretons, it is strange to note, made a distinctly unfavourable impression on him.

---

* *Revue de Paris*, Jan. 15th, 1899.

"The children watching the cattle by the roadside," he observes, "took to flight at our approach, screaming. . . . A party of little girls, catching sight of us, made the sign of the cross, and uttered uncouth cries, in which we thought we heard the word 'Korrigans.' 'Korrigan' it should be said, is the name of the little legendary demons which haunt the Druidical sites of Brittany."

But one of the most interesting revelations of the diary is that young Viaud was by no means as melancholy a being as he afterwards imagined himself to be. He had all a French boy's sense of humour, and rejoiced hugely at such a catastrophe as the collapse of a chair beneath a customer in a tuck-shop.

He was gazetted second-class *aspirant* (junior midshipman, one might translate it) on August 1, 1869. The following October he embarked aboard the *Jean Bart*, Captain A. L. Mottez, for an instructional ocean cruise. The weighing of the anchor should have been a thrilling moment for the young officer. At last, he was to see the wonderful richly-coloured lands beyond the sunset, of which he had dreamed through the long silent summers at Rochefort and Castelnau. But he missed the dramatic value of the moment, and has left no record of it.

During the cruise, three of Loti's comrades died and were buried at sea. Loti's horror of death was intensified. Yet a burial at sea is far less tragic and lugubrious than a funeral on land.

The cruise of the *Jean Bart* was world wide, touching at all the five continents. The principal ports of call were Teneriffe, Gibraltar, Algiers, Malaga, Syracuse, Smyrna, Port Said, Malta, Las Palmas, Bahia, Newport (U.S.A.), Halifax (N.S.) and Brest. From Newport a visit was paid to New York. Midshipman Viaud assisted at the celebration of the Fourth of July, and as we have been told, got drunk for the second time in his life.

The young officer returned to France a writer made. His visions of strange sunburnt lands had been realised; a consciously picturesque figure, he had mingled with Turks and Greeks on the wharves of Smyrna, with darker Arabs in the back streets of Algiers, and penetrated into the green night of the Brazilian forest. If the novel *Matelot* embodies his experiences, we must believe that he found a sweetheart of some sort in every port. The tortoise, Suleiman, which he took back with him to Rochefort was so named after a waif whom he befriended at Oran, and whom he was to meet again on a subsequent visit to North Africa. At Quebec he places the scene of a trivial love-affair with a long-haired Canadian girl, which may or may not have marked his call at Halifax or Newport. Loti's native egotism was quickened by his enlarged experience. Self-expression became an urgent need; and in self-expression, though he was far from realising it at the time, he found his real vocation. As to his style, he wrote as he saw and felt. Probably he thought keeping this diary as good a way as any of passing the long hours between ports—and between love affairs. The historical, artistic, and political physiognomy of the places he saw he was hardly conscious of. Otherwise, he might have written mere travel books.

Shortly after the celebrations at New York the *Jean Bart* was recalled to France in consequence of the outbreak of the Franco-German war. An event of more direct importance to Loti was the death of his father, Jean Theodore Viaud, which occurred in the previous month (June, 1870). To this bereavement, the son, so far as I have been able to trace, devotes no passage.

"A spoilt child—poor physique—no application to his professional interests—has the temperament of an artist." Such was his Commander's report on the *aspirant* Viaud, upon his return from his first ocean cruise. Commandant Mottez was to be congratulated on his discernment.

France, however, had need of officers, and in face of his commander's adverse report, Julien Viaud was promoted first-class *aspirant*. He was posted to the corvette *Decrès*, belonging to a squadron then assembled to menace the German coasts. Admiral Fourrichon, having hoisted his flag on the *Magnanime*, the fleet sailed on August 7.

Operations were confined to a blockade of the coast between the Jahde and the Elbe. The admiral had been forbidden by the government of Napoleon III to bombard unfortified places, and he was not strong enough to attack the forts behind which the infant Prussian fleet had gone to roost. Yet Fourrichon's task was dangerous and difficult enough and called for expert seamanship. Heligoland at that time belonged to the British, so the French ships had to take in coal and supplies outside the three-mile limit on the high seas.

Unfortunately, the pages of Loti's diary covering this, his first experience of war, are missing, except an entry or two describing a friendly reception at Copenhagen; but in a book written many years after,* we find the following recollections of his experiences: "Oh, that long winter of 1870, spent aboard a wretched little boat, cruising in the gales, off the Prussian coast! From my look-out post I used to perceive on the dark horizon the black shape of a certain *König Wilhelm*, which was for ever on our track and before which we always had to run, while her shells burst behind us over the icy water. . . . The misery of realising the futility of our proceedings! News reached us very rarely, under ominous-looking black seals which we broke with a foreboding of disaster. At every reverse, at every recital of German barbarity, we exchanged vows never to forget!"

The weather grew worse and worse—even the elements conspired against France that disastrous autumn—and culminated in a terrific hurricane on September 5. That gale swept the whole Atlantic coast. In it perished the British warship *Captain*, upon the coast of Spain. But Fourrichon's squadron rode out the storm, to return to Cherbourg upon the news of the final catastrophe of Sedan.

The Navy furnished heavy contingents, perhaps the bulk of its personnel, for service with the hard-pressed land forces. But Midshipman Viaud

* *Les Derniers Jours de Pékin* (1902).

remained at sea, cruising in the Channel aboard the *Decrès,* between Cherbourg and Dunkerque, till the end of the war.   Of the glories of a sailor's life he had seen nothing: but, that long dreadful winter on the cold grey Northern seas, he learnt somewhat of the patience and stoical endurance required of the seaman, and faced the seaman's worst enemy in her worst moods.   He was never again to sail in such high latitudes.   So it may be safely asserted that it is to the abortive operations of the French Navy that we owe the realism and most dramatic episodes of *Pêcheur d'Islande.*

CHAPTER IV

THE ISLE OF DESIRE

On March 15, 1871, Loti joined the despatch-boat *Vaudreuil* at Lorient in Brittany. Three days later, the Commune was proclaimed in Paris, and while awaiting the issue of the outbreak, the little vessel cruised between Lorient and Bordeaux. The aimless evolutions, to which the fleet of an essentially land power is for the greater part of its time doomed, must be little short of maddening to men of energetic temperament. But Julien Viaud was hardly one of these, and his newly discovered faculty for writing helped him to pass the time. Besides, there were always girls to see, or that one might hope to see, at the west coast ports.

On May 18, Loti being then twenty-one years old, the *Vaudreuil* sailed from Lorient for the Pacific. En route, the ship lay for six days off Dakar, which our author was to know better later on, and then steered west for Cayenne and the Iles du Salut thence following the South American coast down to the Horn.

This particular cruise gave the occasion for that article entitled "Mes Dernières Chasses," which

33

reflects more honour on Loti than anything else he ever wrote.

While wandering, gun in hand, through an equatorial forest (probably near Bahia), he falls asleep. He is awakened and sees a monkey grimacing at him from a tree. "And moved by one of those aggressive instincts which proceed from the depths of our nature," he puts his gun to his shoulder and murders the harmless, defenceless little animal.

"Then, only, I perceived the stupid hideousness of what I had done. Never had I cursed myself so fervently. 'Brute!' I murmured to myself, between my clenched teeth, 'Stupid brute!'"

It is difficult to understand how the thing happened at all. Loti's nature would seem to render him incapable of such an act of wanton butchery. Horror-stricken by his act, he tells us, he never touched a gun, except when required by the Service, for another five years. Then, in the Isle of Mitylene, he was induced to go shooting birds. He killed no more. And I reproduce here his reflections, not only because they express what was truest and noblest in him, but because they might be addressed with more force to us Englishmen than to the French, especially to those amongst us who pretend to social superiority.

"To think that every day, any number of people— not worse than others, God knows—commit such murders *for pleasure,* go out to amuse themselves by killing, even stowing into their game-bags birds which they have not had the decency to put out of their sufferings. . . . !

"And pigeon shooting! Is there a more ferocious piece of imbecility than this pastime of fashionable snobs?

"And hunting! At the conclusion of an account of one of those killings where the stag weeps—for stags do actually weep when bitten by the dogs—when I fall on the traditional phrase, 'The hoof was presented to the charming Mademoiselle So-and-So,' I picture this young monster, smiling upon another creature's agony, and she appears to me ten times more disgusting than a young Carib gnawing a human bone when urged by hunger."

It would have disgusted the French author even more, perhaps, to hear of the bleeding member of a fox, being presented to an Anglican bishop, as that reverend father in God was journeying to St. Albans. He might also have said something emphatic about the old-fashioned and fashionable practice of "blooding," a form of initiation applied, I believe, even to members of the royal family of this country in their tender years—unless, indeed, his undoubted respect for royalty had stifled the voice of conscience.

He concludes: "In our time, when new and subversive ideas agitate in the smoky air of factories, there are those who dream of suppressing war. War! which chemists, alas! have taken it upon themselves presently to render impossible, but which was the sublime school of abnegation, vigour, and courage. . . .

"But the chase! Is there anyone who can say a word on behalf of the chase, which in ages past had, indeed, its use, its fineness, even a kind of nobility; but which in our days is the preserve of mean and cowardly cruelty?"

So Loti expressed himself in middle-life.* but returning to the journal of his cruise on the *Vaudreuil* we find him denouncing the slaughter of a seal by one of his shipmates, off Cape Horn. "I wanted to be alone with my comrade to tell him what I thought of him, and we had an explanation which very nearly ended in blows." One wishes that it had.

The midshipman was not happy on the *Vaudreuil* and he left it in October without regret at Valparaiso. His commander, notwithstanding, had reported favourably on him—"likely to become a good officer." His cruise on this ship was not very rich in literary fruit, though his description of the desolate regions of the Horn is as vivid as anything he afterwards wrote.

From Loti the novelist to Loti the philanderer is never a long step. At Valparaiso he was introduced to a lady he calls Carmencita. She was about thirty-five years old, a mature age for a Spanish woman. Loti recalls her exquisite eyes, "too long ever to finish," which turned up at the corners, Chinese fashion, when she smiled. At her house, in the quietest residential part of the Chilian city, the young sailor spent all his shore leave. The friendship, he assures us, was quite platonic. Rather, I should say, it belonged to the *pays du tendre*. At

* 1898 *Reflets sur la sombre Route.*

first, he looked upon the Chileña as quite elderly, an old maid, in fact. Then one evening she danced for him one of the native dances of her land, and it seemed to him that she was still young.

Perhaps he regretted his friend a little when, on December 19, he sailed on the admiral's flagship, the frigate *Flore*. At Easter Island, contrary to his unstudious, unscientific habit, he made a serious archæological study of the grotesque monoliths which have so long puzzled the learned. This, accompanied by drawings of his own, he sent to the Paris *Illustration*. At Nukahiva, again, he was busy with pencil and sketch book. One wonders whether it was not originally some idea of appearing to his admiral as a serious, intelligent young officer that threw our midshipman into the ranks of writers.

On January 29, 1872, he sighted the peaks of Tahiti.

In view of the renown conferred on this island by Loti, a renown refreshed in a measure by Gauguin and Somerset Maugham, some readers may be interested to learn that it is in area a little smaller than the county of Surrey. The only town is Papeete. Having been declared a French protectorate as far back as the early 'forties of the last century, Tahiti, in the year 1872, continued nominally under the rule of a native queen, Pomaré.

The spell of the South Sea Isles has drawn other men than Loti from the opposite side of the world. It is a spell not to be felt or understood by everyone. The islands have no history, or none, rather, has been transmitted to us. Their art, though it has recently found admirers, excites the pitying derision of most people. The European finds himself at a tiny spot where nothing has happened or is ever likely to happen. As to the scenery, travellers have told me that there is no diversity and that you soon find it monotonous. The ocean round about has no memories of formidable buccaneers; only very rarely, and within our own time, has the Pacific silence been disturbed by the cannon-thunder of contending fleets. From the mountain tops you descry ships bound only to such uninspiring places as Sydney, Auckland, and San Francisco. The isles of the Pacific might seem to some as little romantic as Kew Gardens.

Not so to Midshipman Viaud, whose fancy they had inflamed in the quiet house at Rochefort. Here within a boat's length was that Arcadia he had dreamed of at his window overlooking the ramparts. Here he was on the track of the brother whom he idealised the more as his memory grew fainter. Was he disappointed? For a moment, he writes in a mood of disillusionment. It is his sister to whom he writes. She was ever his confidante even of his most passionate love passages. "I have been almost all over the world, and at last I behold the island of my dreams. But I have found nothing but melancholy and bitter disappointment.

"And yet it is verily and indeed Papeete; there is the queen's palace, and there among the greenery, the bay shaded by palms, the mountains beyond with their jagged outline—it is all just as I knew it would be. . . . Yes, all that, but minus the charm, the wondrous charm of vague illusions, of childhood's strange and fantastic impressions.

"Besides, the fellows on board have spoiled my Tahiti by picturing it from their point of view. They smear all that is poetical with the slime of mockery, their own dullness and ineptitude. And civilisation has been over busy—our hateful colonial civilisation, with our conventionality, our habits and vices. Wild poetry flies away with the customs and traditions of the past."*

The French officers were presented to Queen Pomarè. "In the massive ugliness of her old age" the midshipman still thought he could trace vestiges of beauty. A crown, even a Polynesian one, always to Loti beautified the face beneath. He was met by one of her majesty's sons, "a tawny colossus in evening dress. . . ." The style of a European Court was pitifully aped by Tahitian royalty. Loti was not altogether blind to its petty vulgarity.

The spell was broken. The dream-island faded out of sight; and then, strange to say, he fell under the spell of the reality. Whatever the child imagined it to be, the man found Tahiti to be the isle of Cytherea, the paradise of the healthy voluptuary. There was nothing here to stir the imagination or the intellect, but everything to soothe, to charm, and to satisfy the senses.

The women of Tahiti are admittedly lovely. They must not be judged, I presume, by the hideous caricatures of Gauguin. And in 1872, before the work of the missionaries had borne fruit, they gave

* *The Marriage of Loti.* Translated by Clara Bell.

their loveliness freely for their own pleasure, or for an inconsiderable reward. Of sexual morality, apparently, the Tahitians had no conception at all. They gratified their passions as a matter of course, as one sleeps or eats. The queen and her subjects were nominally Christians, and conformed so far to European notions of decency as to wear flimsy garments. But modesty, even decency, was unknown. Jealousy, though it must have occurred among them, was not regarded almost as a virtue. Fidelity in sex matters was not expected of man or woman.

The son of the Huguenots of Rochefort found this state of things much to his liking. He says of himself, "While yet very young, Loti had been cast on the stormy tide of European life. At a very early age he had lifted the curtain which hides the drama of the world from infant eyes. Launched at the age of sixteen on the whirlpool of London and Paris, he had suffered at an age when most lads have scarcely begun to think. Loti had withdrawn from this campaign in the dawn of his life, very weary, and believing himself already quite used up. He had been very thoroughly sickened and disappointed because before this change into a youth like other young men, he had been an innocent and dreamy child, brought up in the pure peace of family life."

Well, that, of course, was not quite so. This is plainly an endeavour to disarm the criticism of the readers of the *Nouvelle Revue*. The author by his own confession tasted the fruit of the tree of knowledge not much earlier than most boys of Latin race, and he had not plunged at all deeply into the dissipations of Paris. At Tahiti, it was not a case of idyllic innocence and simplicity refreshing jaded, disillusioned manhood. It was the irresistible appeal of youth unfettered to youth set free—of lovely half-naked girls to a vigorous sensual youth of twenty-two. The love of Loti and Rarahu was the embrace of two healthy young animals.

It is easy, of course, to dismiss this as mere lust, easy to forget that the most romantic, sentimentally-expressed "love" is but a reverberation of the sexual instinct. Loti seems to have been endowed with a keener sensual zest than most men, and to have attained to degrees of sexual rapture denied to the majority. Writing at the other side of the world, vaguely conscious of European standards and sensibilities, he strives to introduce a note of tenderness into a diary of voluptuousness—"he was beginning to love her, really to love her. Far away he wonders what has become of his dusky love, whether she pines for him. . . ."

In actual fact, there was no Rarahu. Or rather there were many. The character is a mere synthesis of the Maori woman, an embodiment of what the girls of the island had meant for the author. This he confesses in a letter dated February 24, 1879—a disturbing disclosure to those travellers who claim to have met the heroine in her old age and talked with her of her French lover. For that matter, in the sketch *Un vieux Collier*,* he relates

* *Le château de la Belle-au-Bois-Dormant.*

another Oceanic amour with almost brutal candour. "This collar of hibiscus flowers belonged to a girl met once upon a time, on a lonely strand in the dusk. I loved her for *the space of an hour.* . . . The twilight, the sadness of the hour, the terrible or desolate aspect of nature, conspired to unite us. We were children, alone and lost, in surroundings all too natural. The terror of the night awoke in us that want which every soul experiences of another soul, and in a more humble, but alas! human order—that desire which every body has of another body, of a body sweet to caress and embrace, to chase away that overpowering sense of loneliness. . . . While nature round about showed herself indifferent and fatal, we exchanged those tendernesses which impart, among the young, something infinitely kind and fraternal to the brutality of love."*

Yet . . . when they withdrew from each other, he felt that they were separated by an abyss of incomprehension, like two beings of different species.

He admits, you see, that no community of speech or thought was necessary to his enjoyment of woman. According to the novel, however, he did acquire a colloquial knowledge of Tahitian. And he was baptised by a Tahitian name.

"Loti was baptised on January 25, 1872, at the age of twenty-two years and eleven days. When the deed was done, it was about one in the afternoon by London and Paris time. On the other side and the other way up of the terrestrial ball, in the gar-

* *Un vieux Collier.*

dens of Queen Pomarè, where the event took place, it was nearly midnight. In Europe it was a cold and dismal winter's day. On the reverse side, in the queen's gardens, it was a calm languorous, enervating summer's night.

"Five persons took part in this ceremony of baptism amidst mimosas and orange-trees, in a fervid and fragrant air, under a sky starry with southern constellations. These five were Ariitea, princess of the blood, Faïmana and Teria, ladies in attendance on her majesty, Plunket and Loti, midshipmen in the royal navy of Great Britain. Loti, who had been hitherto known as Harry Grant, still kept that name in all official documents and on the books of the ship he was attached to; but that of Loti was commonly adopted among his friends.

"The ceremony was simple and performed without much speech or paraphernalia. The three Tahitian girls, who wore crowns of natural flowers and tunics of pink muslin with long skirts, after vainly endeavouring to pronounce such barbarous words as Harry Grant and Plunket—their Polynesian throats. finding the harsh consonants impossible—determined to know the two youths by the names of Remuna and Loti, being those of two flowers. It was further understood that the first words of a native song, 'Loti taïmane,' sung at night, should be understood to convey, 'Loti is here and begs his fair friend to join him'."*

But the writer's real name was Viaud, which could not present any difficulties for the Polynesian

* *The Marriage of Loti.*

throat. For once in a way, therefore, the truth may have been more picturesque than Loti's version, and the name bestowed on him by way of endearment by a Tahitian sweetheart. It is even more likely that he took it upon himself when, for the time being, he discarded European costume and arrayed himself in the *pareo* and simple garments of the islanders. The princess of the blood may have been as fictitious as Plunket and Harry Grant themselves. Seeing that our author affected to hold the English in horror, I find it odd that he should have chosen to masquerade in the pages of his second novel as a British naval officer.

The Pacific Cytherea left a deep impression upon Loti's character and literary imagination, though he stayed there less than two months. The frigate sailed for Honolulu and San Francisco on March 23, calling again at the island at the end of June, and thence proceeding homewards. His readers can believe, if they will, in his anguish at being separated from his Tahitian sweethearts. It was, however, to be expected that, on meeting Carmencita again on the homeward run, the sailor, fresh from the embrace of his dusky paramours, found her strangely worn and faded.

The *Flore* anchored at Brest on December 4, 1872, and was put out of commission. Midshipman Viaud, having touched the Happy Isles, went home. There he found a copy of the *Illustration* of August 17, containing his article on Easter Island, and what purported to be a reproduction of his drawings; but the engraver had taken such liberties with the original sketch that the youth's pleasure in his first published contribution to the Press was completely marred. The original and the reproduction are shown for our comparison in the *Illustration* of April 28, 1923. We are not surprised at Loti's indignation; but the wrong was trifling compared with what writers have had to put up with at the hands of the pestilent brood of illustrators. Smothering his righteous resentment, Loti allowed the Nukahiva drawings to be published in the same journal in September and October, 1873; but oddly enough, when asked to supply an explanatory text, delegated the task to his sister, Mme. Bon.

CHAPTER V

AFRICAN SKIES AND TRAGIC LOVE

WE are not told whether Midshipman Viaud notified his change of name to his family circle. He took advantage of his leave to instal his tortoise at home, and to introduce him to the cat; but the acquaintance thus begun never ripened into anything like friendship.*

Our sailor next appears in the naval manœuvres on the Mediterranean coast. He visits Toulon, Villefranche, and presumably Nice and Monte Carlo, now in full season (February—March, 1873). On this coast he lays the opening scenes of his poor novel, *Matelot*. He has nothing to say about the Riviera resorts. The courtesans of Monte Carlo, with their polonaises and chiffons, had no charms, apparently, for the lover of Rarahu. His stark animalism protected him from the appeal of organised vice.

Homesick for savagery, by pestering the Minister of Marine, he got a ship on the Senegal station. By this time he had been promoted *enseigne de vaisseau* (sub-lieutenant). He sailed on the *Entreprenante*

* *Fleurs d'ennui.*

46

and joined his ship, the despatch-boat, *Pétrel*, off Dakar, on September 21.

Two years before, from the deck of the *Vaudreuil*, he had caught glimpses of West Africa. He knew, therefore, the kind of country he was going to. It could have been no longing for soft sensuous delights that urged him to seek this coast. No sharper contrast could there be than between the delicious southern isle and the harsh frontiers of the desert, tawny as a lion's hide. Here was a different sort of barbarism from the Polynesian. Here nature was hostile to man, and every man's hand was against his neighbour. Near the great rivers, you tread ever upon some old battle ground—farther off, every sand dune hides the bones of a whole caravan.

The Senegal country has been fought over, again and again, by different tribes and races. Here powerful black kings have reigned and built up some barbarous sort of civilisation. Here negro *condottieri* have pulled down such princes from their thrones and reigned for a time in their stead. Even the European who, in other parts of Africa, enters the stage very late, in trousers and topee, here stalks on in the first act, a picturesque figure in coat-of-mail and vizored helmet. For the French established themselves on these shores not long after the murder of Jeanne d'Arc. Some allege that there was an even earlier settlement by the mariners of Dieppe, in the year 1380.

Loti, it is safe to say, recked little of this. He was curiously wanting in the historic sense. But he recognised in St. Louis a city with a past, dying by inches, "with a half-Egyptian look"; at moments it reminded him poignantly of quiet decaying *sous-préfectures* in southern France. A queer, sad place, this, a half mediæval town on a tropical river. . . . Our author conveys to us the sadness, the sternness of this African coast.

"November—this was the fine season, corresponding to our winter at home; the heat was less oppressive, the keen dry wind of the desert had succeeded to the blustering storms of summer.

"When the fine season begins in Senegal, a man may camp with perfect security in the open air, without a roof to his tent. For six months not a drop of rain will fall. Day after day, with pitiless certainty, the land will be scorched beneath a burning, devouring sun.

"Every green thing dies—even the cactus, the prickly nopals, are blighted and their melancholy yellow blossoms wither. A sad depressing autumn that brings with it neither the long cheerful evenings of Europe nor the charm of the first fruits of the year, an autumn that has no harvest of the fields, no golden fruitage of the orchards. Never a fruit in this God-abandoned land. Not even the date palm yields a crop here. Nothing ripens, nothing but the ground-nuts and the bitter pistachios.

"The feel of winter, experienced in the midst of still torrid heat, impresses the imagination strangely."

Elsewhere, we read:

"Winter skies there are even in Africa, seldomer it is true than with us, but all the more strange and sinister in that desolate land. One vast cloud covered the heavens, so black and lowering, that the plain beneath looked white. The desert seemed an endless snow-clad steppe."*

Here we have one aspect of West Africa, and the least familiar. Farther south, the *Pétrel* calls at the mouth of the Mellacorée in French Guinea. Loti lands, pays his respects to Miss Mary Parker, the negro queen of these parts, and penetrates to the stifling recesses of the jungle. At Hafandi, the French officers are received by Babu Mongil, a local chief, and assist at a festival. "Arrives a troop of children from three to four years of age, all of a pretty reddish-brown colour, very shiny and round. They execute, to the music of the tom-tom, a most complicated dance with studied attitudes and the gravity of grown persons."

He draws the portrait of the titular king of Dakar and makes excursion into the desert with a party of the formidable and mysterious Tuareg. His curious fondness for dressing up is again gratified. He wears the *burnous* and veil of the desert riders and is greeted like them with respectful fear by the negro population. Without these expeditions he would die of boredom. He dines at Dakar with two marine lieutenants and a subaltern in the Tirailleurs—this last an Austrian prince ruined at the age of twenty. "You might seek a long way for four people more different and who get on so well together; yet never was a dinner more dismal, nor conversation more lugubrious. . . . Extravagant distractions in the street concluded the evening.

* *The Sahara* (English translation of the *Roman d'un Spahi*).

The most successful was organising a concert of barking dogs at the door of the Governor. At midnight, hailed the *Pétrel* from a deserted quay."

At this moment, Loti was drawing near to what the romantic would call the love of his life; for romance lies rather in desire than fulfilment, in frustration rather than in satisfaction. M. Serban, in the first edition of his biography, cleverly inferred from certain passages in his hero's well-known novels, that Loti had once in his life been genuinely, deeply, and unhappily in love, in the established European fashion; and this inference was afterwards confirmed by the publication of *Un Jeune Officier Pauvre* in 1923. Under date December, 1873, Loti records an excursion of pleasure to a spot which reminded him of La Limoise, inland from Dakar. "With us there were three Frenchwomen of Dakar. . . . The ladies who accompany us, although Créoles,* have long fair curls, little hats of crepe, and elegant black dresses."

One of these women may have been the woman whom Loti was to love. Certainly, there is no mention of love-making by him on this particular occasion, but the entry concludes on an unwontedly sentimental note. Loti in these out-of-the-way regions has encountered an old medico, whom he supposed to have been in love with his mother. "It was," he muses, "at the romantic epoch when, by reason of an unfortunate love, a whole life might be ruined. To-day we find it hard to understand

---

* Perhaps it is well to remind the reader that a Créole is not necessarily a half-breed or mulatto.

such sentiments; they seem to us even a trifle ridiculous, because we are too sceptical and blasé."

He was soon to understand then, himself, well enough. The lady has been identified by M. Serban, I know not on what authority, with the wife of a high colonial functionary. That our naval officer by this time found himself imperiously in need of a love affair, we cannot doubt; and even in the eyes of so fervent a nature-worshipper, a French woman of culture must have compared favourably with the wiry-haired, shiny black African beauties. Loti's impressions of the skies and plains of Senegal were permanently coloured by the disappointment which ensued. Under date May, 1874, we read: "At five in the afternoon we left St. Louis. The sun was going down. Swiftly we were borne down the yellow river. As I passed the *Pétrel*, my friends waved to me. My heart ached at leaving them. And then behind us receded into the distance the mournful white town of St. Louis, with its sands and thin yellow palm trees. So I lost sight of that corner of Africa, where I had so deeply loved and so deeply suffered."

Transferred to the *Espadon*, he found the tranquillity overwhelming, after the violent emotions of those last days at St. Louis. But he took particular note of his cabin, for "when the heart is filled with an intense passion, the least details of external objects impress themselves on the mind." In another place, he speaks of a great tree among the sandhills of Dakar, under which he stationed himself to watch the ship taking his well-beloved back to France. "That day a high wind was shaking the giant tree overhead, and lashing the water over which the ship was speeding into enormous waves. It was at the noonday heat. The sun beat upon my forehead and my shoulders, but I felt nothing. . . ."

Later, on the eve of his own departure from Africa, he returned to the same spot. But whatever charm the desert might once have had for him was now utterly gone. His thoughts had pursued his loved one to France.

His love so far had been unfortunate or frustrate, but he was not without hope. The scene changes to Savoy. Thence by diligence he travels over the mountains till, far below in the plain, he sees the lights of a great city. Presently the wheels grate on the paved streets, where busy passers-by move through the mist.

"This was the city to which I had come, alone and a stranger (foreigner?), to make a last desperate overture—it struck me as infinitely dreary.

"I wandered along the quays, inquiring for the hotel where I expected to find letters. The hotel was crowded with Russians and English, tourists whose gaity rang harshly in my ear. Supper was served. I could not swallow a mouthful.

"About nine o'clock I went out, having asked the way. The night was dark, the mist was thick. To one coming straight from luminous Africa, the effect was heart-breaking. I continued a long time along streets steep, sombre, and deserted. At last I came to the house which I sought—an old aristocratic mansion with escutcheons carved on its door.

"I trembled like a child before that door. No light, no sound proceeded from the house wherein I was to stake my life's chances . . . I raised my hand to the knocker. I became dizzy, I could hardly breathe . . ."

At this point a note advises us that several pages of the diary are missing. There can be no hesitation about identifying the city with Geneva.

Loti returns to Annecy, and announces to the faithful sailor who awaits him, "All is over. Finish your work and come with me. I fear to be alone." In the classic phrase, he had loved and lost. For several months following, the diary registers his anguish and remorse. Like all unhappy lovers, he hugs his sorrow and dreads nothing so much as forgetfulness—for the pain he suffers belongs to Her, is all of Her that he now possesses. He is ill with a *maladie de chagrin*, close akin to the brain-fever of English novels. He seeks forgetfulness or an anodyne in pleasure, in gay society, and finds it not.

That is practically all we know about the great author's love tragedy. M. Serban takes it very seriously indeed, and compliments the sufferer on his manly reticence. The extracts given strike me as rather in the vein of Alfred de Musset; but we have M. Samuel Viaud's assurance at the beginning of the book that this "is only an intimate journal, never written with a view to publication, and with many pages missing." The story is easily re-constructed. The young lieutenant, thrown,

in the limited circles of the colony, into constant touch with the pretty wife of the high
official, falls deeply in love with her and she, perhaps, was more or less in love with him. Fate
or the husband intervened. She was sent back
to France, holding out hopes of a future meeting
to her sailor. He followed sooner probably than
she expected, traced her to Geneva, and made
a desperate appeal to her either to elope with him
or to accept him as her lover. He was turned away
from her door, for the time being, heart-broken.
(And I can imagine no more dispiriting place on such
an occasion than Geneva in winter).

Loti's passion for dramatising himself on all
possible occasions makes one a little suspicious. . .
But when a man is a poet, he naturally expresses
his sentiments poetically, even when he is writing
for himself, or rather his future self, alone. He did
not use this particular love affair as literary material;
either because he held it too sacred, or because it
paled in comparison with other and later passions,
To his tragical experience of the European woman,
we may also ascribe, if we like, the preference he was
to evince in future for women of other civilisations.

This unnamed She, the *Bien-aimée*, is not to be
sought for in the lurid pages of *The Sahara* (*Roman
d'un Spahi*). Nor would M. Serban allow us to
confound her with the seductive mulatto Cora, the
Messalina of St. Louis. Yet Cora is described as a
half-caste with hair of red blonde, as elegantly
dressed, and the wife of a rich merchant trading
on the river. This likeness is near enough to that

of the ladies who went with Loti on that country excursion to make us wonder whether the author, healed of his wound, did not create the character in order to revenge himself upon the woman who had hurt him.

The central episode of the romance seems, at any rate, to be founded on fact. Cora, we read, "lived in a huge rambling house, brick-built, and with the half-Egyptian look the buildings have in the older quarters of St. Louis. It was all glaringly white as an Arab caravan serai. On the ground-floor, vast open courtyards, where the Moors of the desert camped with their camels on the sand, and an odd miscellany of cattle, dogs, ostriches, and negro slaves swarmed. Above—endless verandahs, supported by massive square pillars, like the terraces of ancient Babylon.

"The living apartments were reached by outside staircases of white stone, of monumental proportions. All this, dilapidated and dreary, like everything else in St. Louis.

"The great reception hall had a certain air of grandeur. Its furniture was of the 17th century. Blue lizards haunted it, cats and parrots and gazelles chased each other across the fine-woven mats from the Guinea coast; negro women crossed it, with indolent gait, leaving behind them, musky savours. The whole place breathed an indescribable atmosphere of sadness and solitude and exile; it was dreary, dreary, especially at evening when the noises of the day had ceased and the African breakers played their everlasting dirge."

Here Cora's lover, the Spahi, Jean Peyral, surprises her with her new lover—a young man, almost a boy, in a naval uniform—Loti, of course. Then, according to pages of the diary seen by M. Serban, the soldier sent a respectfully worded challenge to the officer, inviting him to meet him at the recognised duelling ground near the cemetery of Sorr. Loti appeared at the appointed time, but instead of fighting, the two men exchanged confidences and condolences. And the Spahi became the hero of his rival's romance, written six or seven years after. For Jean Peyral's home in the Cevennes, the author drew upon his recollection of Bretenoux.

CHAPTER VI

JOLLY JACK TAR

LOTI had returned to France in September, 1874. He had earned the commendation of his superiors. He was reported on as "intelligent, full of zeal and goodwill, an excellent subordinate," and later, "has made an excellent beginning and promises to be a most valuable officer." The sun of Senegal seems to have dried up and hardened much that was flabby in the young man's nature. The desert wind acted as a tonic after the tepid baths of Polynesia. Loti had become a real sailor, enjoying his job. The *Espadon* had made rough weather. He recalls, the "constant danger, the furious gale, the high seas, the uncertainty, and withal, the consciousness of one's duty accomplished . . . the ceaseless responsibility, the absolute necessity of devoting every one of my faculties to the common good." And that, while he was devastated by passion, by a fever of hope and fear.

His first serious disappointment in love, perhaps also the encouraging notice of his commanding officers, strengthened his attachment to his profession. He entered for a year's course at the

School of Physical Training and Fencing at Joinville sur Pont, just outside Paris, near Vincennes. Hard exercise and lively companionship inevitably pushed his unhappy love-affair into the background of his consciousness. The British officer undergoing training would look with envy and certainly with surprise on the license enjoyed by him and his comrades. At Joinville, Loti was introduced to the sort of society he had found stale and unprofitable while a homesick youth in the Quartier. He lodged in an ugly house opposite the station reserved for officers following the course. Every officer had his mistress either living with him or paying him frequent visits. Loti appears to have been an exception. For this reason, perhaps, his favour was courted by the girls, especially, he tells us, by Henriette and her friend, Berthe. They bombarded him with flowers when he appeared on his balcony; when he shut his door, they came in by the window; one night, they invaded his bedroom and had to be driven out with blows. "Impossible to sleep before two o'clock in the morning," he groans, "the nights that Henriette comes to Joinville!"

He would not, perhaps, have driven away the charming Fratine, the *amie* of his friend Delguet, a shop-girl of the Mimi Pinson type. He liked her originally because she came from Savoy, and therefore, to the exaggerated sensibilities of a lover, exhaled somewhat of the fragrance of his now dying passion. She plays a curious part in the last act of that drama. In June, 1875, Loti writes to Delguet from Annecy, announcing that he is obliged to return to X. (by which he means Geneva), "though, no doubt (*sic*), the cruellest disappointment awaits" him. He adds that he hasn't a halfpenny, but can trust to luck to find his way back. Whether he went to "X" or not, a week later, we find him at Annecy in the company of "la petite Fratine," who had lately returned to her country! A happy coincidence, truly. At the end of a delightful day passed in the woods and on the mountains, they kissed and parted.

Our sailor thoroughly enjoyed the life at Joinville. He noticed not only the girls, but his landlady's cat and three dogs, for which I like him better. The evenings were spent at an estaminet, where officers and N.C.O's changed clothes, drank and hobnobbed together. "Every Sunday evening (we read) we have the diverting spectacle of Parisian excursionists running like mad to catch the last train home from Joinville. At our balcony, in front of the station, we see all the fun. We occasionally amuse ourselves by pelting the most belated wretches with eggshells, asparagus stalks, and other odds and ends from our supper table. This makes our victims very wild, and torn between the desire of vengeance and fear of losing their train, they stop to shake their fists at us, then run more frantically than ever, which delights us hugely."

Loti had a nice taste for contriving amusement. As a child, he used to drop letters of the most mystifying and sensational character in the street, and then enjoy, from his window, the horrified bewilderment of the passer-by who picked them up.

This is a form of practical joke from which Loti's present biographer once upon a time extracted considerable amusement; but his letters generally declared in harrowing terms, that the supposed writer (someone well-known in the district) was about to commit suicide by hanging in his back attic. The cream of the joke, I should add, consisted in seeing the finder of the letter invoke the attention of the police, and in following the officer to the very door of the house where the tragedy was alleged to have taken place.

Second-Lieutenant Viaud did justice both to himself and his instructors at Joinville. He left the school in the middle of 1875, enormously pleased with his physical development and athletic skill, but disappointed, so he long afterwards wrote, that he had not become more beautiful! Indeed, if certain passages in *Un Jeune Officier Pauvre* are to be taken as actual biography, he seems for a time to have aspired to the reputation of a terrible fellow, a veritable desperado. Awaiting orders at Rochefort, he found the old home distinctly dull. He frequented the lower class estaminets and was accounted the leader of a rowdy gang of seamen, "who were at heart, honest fellows." With a characteristic touch, he adds, "I hold them in the hollow of my hand, and they would follow me through the flames." They made a row, he admits, but their fists only battered the faces of those who deserved it. For some years, till, in fact, he got his next step in rank, our hero was very fond of disguising himself as an ordinary seaman and conducting himself generally as 'Jack ashore.' As he never got drunk, this uproariousness must have been rather difficult to sustain.

Only by such extravagances, Loti wants us to believe, could he lull the ache of his broken heart. (I am sure he had been reading de Musset). "Here in my old home, where every object recalls the past, the frightful reality is plainly visible to me. A mortal anguish has seized me, and I understand that my life is irretrievably ruined."

The contrast between Rochefort and Joinville must have been sharp indeed. Orders to join the *Couronne* (armoured frigate) at Toulon had a remarkable tonic effect. The heartiness of his appetite astonished his family. He showed a seaman-like alacrity in obeying the order to report at once.

At Toulon, he had a very good time. The bruised heart was temporarily forgotten. He placed his musical talent at the disposal of a benevolent society which organised concerts for the benefit of the poor. At the head was "an old maritime lady" who, with her daughter, introduced the new lieutenant to the society of the station. One day, when he had not ten francs in his pocket, he took a chance at the tables (possibly at Monte Carlo, not far off) and was so far favoured by fortune that he was able to furnish his cabin in a fashion of which he was justly proud. The letters he writes at this time are positively cheerful. They include two to his friend "Plunkett." Who this person was, I have not yet discovered. He was certainly no Englishman; for no Englishman would spell his name in such a fashion and no Englishman ever succeeded in writing such French.*

Loti's stay at Toulon is marked by an episode which, if transferred to the pages of a novel, would be dismissed by any English reader as preposterous and incredible. This officer in the navy performs at his own station as a clown in a public circus and invites his friends to the show. One fails to imagine even Mr. Midshipman Easy, after a night out, so far forgetting the dignity of the service. M. Serban is not at all concerned with his hero's loss of dignity. He sees only in the display an exhibition of Loti's growing vanity and eccentricity. It was a snobbish thing, too, he considers, to invite his swell acquaintances. Oddest of all, it seems to me, is that one, who liked to fancy himself a Byron or a Blighted Corsair, should masquerade as a clown!

As such, he scored a sensational success. Next day he found his cabin full of bouquets, oranges, and cardboard cats, thrown into the ring by his enthusiastic admirers. Most gratifying of tributes was the frank and unstinted praise of the professional mountebanks. They complimented him on his magnificent proportions and marvelled that he, an amateur, should beat them at their own game. "What a pity it is that you are not one of us!" With a certain complacence, Loti admits, he contemplated the muscular frame which exercise had perfected. Not less grateful was the thinly-veiled admiration of the circus ladies who contended for

* M. Samuel Loti Viaud informs me that this was in fact the nom-de-plume of an officer who prefers to remain pseudonymous.

the honour of appearing with him . . . etc., etc.

I wonder if the Admiral heard about it.

Mme. Viaud, in a letter dated Rochefort, May 1st, 1876, found it impossible to congratulate her son upon his parsley crown. These Isthmian or Thespian triumphs were not those which she had wished for him. But she praises him on another count. "Why, my dear child, do you take the trouble to send me an account of your expenses? I have no criticism to offer, I assure you. I imagine that few young men launched in the world spend as little as you, and I shall never cease to deplore the heavy burdens laid upon you."

From later extracts from his diary, we gather that Loti had it very much at heart to discharge all debts contracted by his late father and family. Apparently, he had begun the good work already. A tender, motherly jealousy is revealed in the same letter:

"I cannot help worrying a little when you conceal anything from me; but from another point of view, I am so pleased to see you confide in your sister that I am far from complaining of your letters to her."

So we see Julien Viaud, at the age of twenty-six, unable to resist a pretty girl, posing to himself as the blighted heart-broken lover, and clowning in a circus; stinting himself to redeem the honour of his family, thinking ever of his home, bosom friends with his mother and sister. He was very much a Frenchman.

CHAPTER VII

THE GREEN-EYED CIRCASSIAN

WE reach the most romantic chapter in Loti's life.

1876 was the year of the Bulgarian atrocities. The chronic unrest in the Balkans was effervescing furiously and the Turks were making strenuous efforts to subdue it. Public opinion in France was less excited than in England. Then, the Turks with their peculiar genius for putting themselves in the wrong, murdered the French consul at Salonica.

The circumstances were interesting, even romantic. At an unlucky moment, a Bulgarian girl arrived at the city, announcing that she had embraced Islam. The Muslims were delighted, the Christians proportionately displeased. The convert or renegade having abruptly and mysteriously vanished, the Turks naturally suspected the Nazarenes of having made away with her. Crowds of true believers invaded the Government house, calling on the Pasha to avenge this insult to the faith. At this juncture, the French and German consuls thought fit to show themselves. The cry went up that the girl was concealed at the German consulate. The German, accompanied by his French colleague, made his way

64

home as quickly as he could, but was followed by the enraged mob, who murdered both consuls just as the Bulgarian girl chose to put in an appearance once more.

In consequence of this event, France despatched a squadron to Turkish waters. The *Couronne*, belonging to this fleet, with Loti on board, left Hyères on May 8th, reaching Salonica eight days later.

His first experience in the land he was to love so well was disagreeable, even macabre. He was ordered to take a body, sewn up in a sack, out into the bay, and to throw it overboard, unseen by the Turks. "I got back," he says, "at four in the morning, the boat full of water, drenched myself, and pretty well fed up with my trip and my late shipmate."

Another lugubrious duty claimed him. The presumed assassins (probably selected at random from the crowd) having been hanged or rather strangled, the bodies of the dead consuls were publicly honoured Loti, with no particular emotion, assisted at one of these solemn acts of humiliation to which weak states have so often of late years been condemned. After a solemn funeral service, the bodies were paraded all round the city, escorted by detachments of French and German sailors, and followed by the Ottoman authorities, the officers of the various foreign warships in the harbour, and the whole consular body. The streets were lined with Turkish soldiers with fixed bayonets. The populace looked on, realising that their nation was performing an act of compulsory penance in the eyes of the world.

"It would have been enough for this crowd to close in on us, to annihilate us," says Loti. "Twice there was a panic. The tail of the procession was pressed too closely by the curious—there was some rough handling and an exchange of blows. The sailors lunged with their bayonets. Everyone thought this was the spark which would produce the general conflagration. But, thanks to the Sultan's police, the danger was averted."

But the Mohammedans did not relax their hostility towards the foreigners, who were preparing the dismemberment of their empire. Men from the squadrons in the bay were forbidden to go ashore without their arms. Sub-lieutenant Viaud wandered into the more retired parts of the ancient city. The streets were deserted. Only at rare intervals a turbaned figure came along hugging the wall.

The sailor stopped by the closed door of a mosque, to watch a couple of storks. At that moment, with a shock, he found that he was being observed— observed by a pair of sea-green eyes from between the stout iron bars of a harem window.

The eyes were large and beautiful, the eyebrows above slightly arched and almost joined. They belonged to a girl, closely veiled, in a Turkish robe of green silk. In presence of a Turk, she would have looked away; but for her a *giaour* was more an object of curiosity than a man. Loti's eyes met hers.

That girl was Hadije,* immortalised as Aziyade,

---

* In the diary I make out the name to be Hakije; but the above spelling seems to be correct.

the subject of Loti's earliest, and in this writer's opinion, most beautiful novel.

By what means, the young officer, one of the strangers who were threatening Islam with formidable engines of destruction, established an understanding with the unknown, we are not specifically told. But he was rigged out presently in complete Albanian costume by certain Jewesses, and to their good offices he may have been indebted for an introduction. Go-betweens of this sort apparently do a thriving trade in Mohammedan communities. Somewhat later on, the daring Frank found a more loyal and reliable intermediary in "Samuel," whose real name was Daniel, a boatman belonging to the colony of Spanish-speaking Jews so long settled at Salonica. It was the girl, not Loti, who first showed a desire to establish something more than erotic relations between them. One night to Loti's "astonishment," she signified her wish to converse with him by means of Daniel. "Till that night, although united a whole month in an intoxication of the senses," they had not been able to exchange a single idea or learn anything about each other. Loti was content, we see, to reduce the relations between man and woman to their simplest terms.

After answering her childish questions as to his parentage, age, country, religion, etc., he elicited some facts about herself. She was a Circassian girl, brought in her tender years to Constantinople, and sold to an aged Osmanli, who intended her for his son. But the son died and the father also, and, at the age of eighteen, she passed into the hands of her actual possessor, a man whom Loti calls Abeddin-Effendi.

This old gentleman, we read elsewhere, was always away from home. Hadije, who seems to have been a slave or concubine, proposed to her giaour lover that they should drown themselves. Instead, as we are told in the book, they spent whole nights locked in each other's arms, in a boat floating on the waters of the gulf. Daniel at first had scruples about his share in this intrigue, but devotion to the Frankish officer converted him into a most efficient accomplice.

When Loti was transferred to the gunboat, *Gladiateur*, stationed off Constantinople, the Jew followed him, and the Circassian girl held out hopes of meeting him there. At Constantinople, Lieutenant Viaud spent all his time ashore, except when on duty. So his commander tells us; but his journal left us in no doubt about that. At Salonica, the Frenchman was in love with the Turkish girl; at Stamboul with Turkey. Certainly, in all the world no place has a more romantic appeal than the city by the Bosporus. Its very aspect combines in a manner absolutely unique, the charm of the East, of the mediæval and the legendary world. I speak, of course, of Constantinople as Loti knew it and as I knew it, under the reign of Abd-ul-Hamid, prior to the modernisation, and possibly the vulgarisation, of Turkey. As late as twenty years ago, it was still potent, this spell which Islam laid upon the French lieutenant for all his life.

We know from his not very coherent narrative that he took a little house for himself in the most

Turkish quarter of the city, and lived in the intervals which his duties permitted, the life, as he conceived it, of a Turk. We know, also, that he beguiled the tedium of waiting for the beloved by a succession of fugitive and somewhat contemptible amours. He liked the country and its people so well that he displayed an unwonted interest in public affairs. He chronicles the accession of Abd-ul-Hamid and the promulgation of the first Ottoman constitution. But though he conveys the atmosphere and the peculiar fascination of the place as no other writer has done, he has not a word to say about its monuments or historic sites. I doubt if he mentions St. Sophia, the most wonderful church in Europe; if he walked round those age-old walls, many towered, which shut off the imperial city even from the sea, he has left no record of his impressions. Never was traveller so little of a tourist. In youth, at least, at each new place, he set himself to absorb its atmosphere, to understand its spirit, to become a part of it; so inevitably, he regarded its "sights" with the indifference of a native. Dickens does not interrupt his narrative to give us his impressions of St. Paul's.

The air of Stamboul, no doubt, fostered Loti's melancholy humour and inclined him to introspection; but "Aziyade," like his Polynesian novel was ultimately composed some years after the events described and under the influence of very different surroundings. Some of the emotions and reflections expressed in the book, notably those embodied in the letters to and from his sister, belong to the later period. It was only in retrospect and not while waiting for his Circassian mistress that he could have written, "I have loved only one woman more than her, and that woman I have no longer the right even to see."

Hadije, as we know, came to Constantinople—I will not say that otherwise the novel would not have been written, for the hero would assuredly have found another and an appropriate heroine! The story of that dark and historic winter is substantially the story of every unfortunate love. All who have loved passionately and unhappily find something strangely reminiscent in Loti's pages. Memories of many bitter partings in circumstances similar or vastly dissimilar, must be poignantly awakened by such passages as this:

"A pale, March sun is setting on the Sea of Marmora. The air at sea is keen and cold. The shores, melancholy and bare, recede into the evening haze. God! is it all finished, then, and shan't I see her any more?

"Stamboul is out of sight now. The loftiest cupola of the loftiest mosque—everything has faded into the distance, everything has disappeared from view. If I could only see her for one moment . . . I would give my whole life just to touch her hand. I am sick for the sight of her.

"For I adore her. All passion apart, with a love the purest and tenderest. I love her soul and her heart which are mine. My love for her will outlast youth, outlast the power of the senses, endure into that mysterious future which brings old age and death.

"This calm of the sea, this pale, March sky, weigh on my heart. God, how I suffer!—as much as if I'd seen her die."

He looks across the Sea of Marmora and sees beyond that vague horizon. "She is in her harem, now, my beloved, in some chamber of that sombre, barred house, lying exhausted, speechless, tearless, awaiting the coming of night. . . . "

And the vessel was headed towards the Dardanelles and France.

So closed an experience which had this distinctive importance. It implanted in Loti a sympathy for Islam above all other religions and made him its friend for ever. We may wonder at this. Some lovers would have been disposed to regard the Circassian odalisque as the victim of Muslim institutions. But apart from her environment he could not conceive her, and certainly would not have cared for her. Aziyade for him was Turkey and Turkey Aziyade.

He winds up the novel, as he winds up the Tahitian story, by killing his heroine and hero. In point of fact, Hadije lived some years after their parting. The sequel to the romance is to be found in the diary published in 1923.

War had broken out between Russia and Turkey. Osman Pasha astonished the world by his defence of Plevna, Gurko not less by his passage of the Balkans. The Turkish resistance crumbled. Before long the Russians were encamped on those bleak, cream-coloured shores of Thrace which Loti had watched fading away in the spring twilight.

Writing on March 2nd, 1878, the French naval officer expresses a half-regret that he did not accept an offer to enter the Ottoman service. It is already only a half-regret, for he sees that his fortunes would then have been joined to those of a sinking ship. From Hadije he receives from time to time smudgy, incoherent little letters in Turkish, entreating him not to abandon her. She had been badly compromised during their last month together at Stambul, and her position has become intolerable. Daniel has returned to Salonica, where he has become what he was before, "a poor devil of a boatman without a halfpenny or a rag to clothe him." But Kedi bey, Loti's cat at Constantinople, is luckier, he has entered the church, has been adopted by the dervishes at the mosque, and is assured of shelter and a supply of mice for the rest of his days. A church cat's position, we see, is very different from a church mouse's. Meanwhile, the house at Eyub, the bower of Loti's love, had been burnt down, as Turkish houses are every, two or three months.

On March 7th, another letter from his Turkish mistress reached him. "A desperate letter, a solemn appeal to my vows, to my pity, to my love." Her lord, old Abeddin, has gone to fight the Muscovites. Being old, brave, and fanatical, he will certainly be killed. She will then have no choice but to marry Osman Effendi of Ghedik-Pasha, who has got a job well behind the line and will not be killed. He is young, audacious, and jealous. Hadije implores Loti to save her.

In reply to this appeal, he writes to a person at Constantinople named Pogarritz, giving him instructions how to find the girl and put her aboard a French steamer bound for Marseilles. Funds for this purpose have been lodged with a secretary at the French embassy. "Lieutenant Viaud cannot come himself—that would amount to desertion, and he has to consider his honour as a French officer, which is dearer to him than he had at first suspected." "On my honour," he concludes, "I swear to you that Aziyade, once in France, shall become my wife."

Did he want her to come? I doubt it. Enclosed in the letter to Pogarritz was another to her, which it had taken him half a day to compose in Turkish. After protesting his love, he strongly recommends her to remain with the good old man who loves her, also, and in the event of his death—to marry Osman Effendi! "He also is rich and he loves you; with him you will be happy. Forget Loti who brings unhappiness to everybody who comes in contact with him. With Osman Effendi, you will have slaves, gardens, rank above the women of your nation, and a wife's position in the invisible world of the harem. Whereas with me!" . . . and the writer draws a graphic picture of the misery which would be hers as the wife of a poor man in a Christian country, adding of course, that if she is prepared to face it, he will make all arrangements for her flight and will welcome her with joy. A good many idylls have furnished on that note.

The letter, we are informed, was written in Turkish. It was written so well that Hadije, simple as she was, read between the lines and stayed at Constantinople. It does not appear that he ever heard from her again.

He had already finished his first novel, and his literary conscience alone forbade him to turn "Aziyade" into Madame Julien Viaud. Before this, he tells us that only his love for his mother prevented his accepting a position offered him in Turkey. He believed himself to be sincere, but it is significant that when he became rich, and was free to do as he liked, he did not settle in the East, Near or Far. Like other Frenchmen, Loti did not regard romance as a sound basis for one's establishment in life. Before receiving what he describes as Aziyade's "tragic letter" of March 7th, he forsaw that some day someone else might wait for him at home, someone, an unknown, whose existence he was unaware of, who might bear him children.

"Could I love them," he asks, "children which would not be yours as well as mine?"

CHAPTER VIII

Upon his return to France, in May, 1877, Viaud was appointed to the despatch-boat *Bouvet* at his home port, Rochefort. While history was making in the country of his affections, he furnished his room in his father's house in Turkish fashion, sat smoking his narghile and dreaming of Constantinople.

He was interrupted by a succession of tedious and exacting duties. His plans for a visit to Paris were upset. "I have lost," he complains, "two of my old comrades of the Naval School, each of whom leaves a void in my existence. I have also lost and buried in a corner of the garden my beloved black and white cat, the companion of my travels."

In September we find him at Lorient, aboard the coast-defence vessel, *Tonnerre*. "Nothing to do here," he grumbles. Brittany was tolerable in the autumn, but winter brought the "rain, the fog, the leafless trees, in fact, the dismal Breton winter, and the inevitable furnished apartment, cold and depressing. He was hard-up; his friends did not appreciate him." He has made, however, two good

75

friends—one a rich old maid, "intelligent and dis-tinguée, of uncertain age, but with great pretentions to youth"; the other, Yves Kermadec, (his real name was Pierre Le Cor)* "a quartermaster of my own age and an old shipmate.

"Of the two (he continues) Yves is of course my favourite. I prefer people who have been allowed to follow their own bent to half-educated people like my colleagues. And, moreover, it is pleasant to have for a comrade one who swallows all your ideas with admiration and regards you as a man of genius."

That preference had become firmly rooted in the sub-lieutenant. It is very marked in him, this liking for the society of the simple and uneducated. His explanation is frank enough, but I suspect that the predilection had been strengthened by his long association with even more primitive folk, such as the Rarahus and Hadijes.

To those dull days at the Breton port he owed fame and fortune. In himself as a literary man Loti took singularly little interest. He does not seem anywhere to have recorded the beginning of his first novel or to have announced his determination to make money by his pen. In a letter dated January 30th, 1878, a friend V.L. . . . tells him he has read his manuscript which, he thinks, is sure of success if published. The inference is that wearied by his life at Lorient, Loti fell back more and more on his memories at Stamboul. Re-

---

* When editing his diaries for publication, Loti generally alters the real names of persons to those he has given to them in his romances.

reading and re-touching his diary, the idea came to him at last to make a book of it. We should be thankful that just at that moment no fresh love affair occurred to overcloud those memories.

It does not appear that he found any particular pleasure at this stage in actual literary work. He was not like those fortunate novelists who tell us that they find their greatest happiness in their work—a happiness, it is to be feared, occasionally out of all proportion to that which they procure their readers. Never dreaming of the brilliant future which was opening before him, Loti gloated over the hollowness of existence. "For him, there is no hope in this world ; he believes in nothing, no one ; he loves nothing, no one; he has no faith and no hope." Making due allowance for the climatic influences of Brittany, his mother and sister at Rochefort were seriously alarmed by his avowed scepticism in the matter of religion. They were even more alarmed on hearing that the pendulum had swung the other way and that the only son of the family proposed to become a Papist and a Trappist monk. Poor dears, they did not realize, of course, that every man of Loti's temperament falls in love with the Catholic church at one time or another in his life as surely as he falls in love with some woman. Only those born in the fold of that church are immune from this infatuation. With Loti it was not very long lived.

Somewhere near Lorient he had discovered a monastery of the Trappist order. "I experienced," he writes in February, 1878, "a singular emotion

77

upon crossing this sombre threshold, which is like the threshold of death. Long have I dreamed of this refuge of the despairing, of this absolute monastic calm." A few days later he obtained hospitality from the community, and stayed two or three days. The other guests, he found, were delinquent priests undergoing a disciplinary course. He talked with the Prior, assisted at the midnight office, and found the monastic life not at all to his taste. Even sleep, the supreme consolation of the unfortunate, was denied to the Trappists. They pretended to be happy, but he saw that they were not. He had much time for meditation, and the result of his meditations he communicated to his sister in these words: "I tell myself that youth soon goes, that time flies quickly, and that the hours we shall have together are already counted—it behoves us then not to lose one of them since we find them precious." He leaves the monastery with "a singular yearning for noise, movement, and liberty. It was almost beautiful in the woods. I ran down the road like a child, singing and leaping the ditches. I thoroughly enjoyed smoking cigarettes and drinking good cider in the village inns."

Our author's flirtation with Catholicism was soon over. It hardly deserved the long, eloquent and controversial letter which Mme. Bon (his sister) had addressed him. Loti's scepticism, at least, was no pose. He never succeeded in believing in a personal God or in a post-mortem existence. But he never formally forsook the Huguenot communion, out of respect for his ancestors and his beloved mother.

His friend Yves took him off for a holiday to his native village. Loti disguised as a mere "rating" spent an enjoyable four days among the Breton fisher-folk, and perhaps then first conceived the strong sympathy with them to be expressed in his most popular novel. Meanwhile, friends had been busy about his manuscript in Paris. Upon his return to Lorient he was advised by telegram that *Aziyade* had been accepted by Calmann-Levy. He went to Paris and suitably celebrated this first success. He received five hundred francs (£20) in advance of royalties, which was not so bad. It was the price which Michel Lévy had paid Flaubert for *Madame Bovary*. At the dinner he met his old friend, the Fratine of the Joinville days. When he spoke to her of Annecy, she showed emotion. "As though her love for me was not extinct, she averted her face and kissed her little child."

Not even the immediate prospect of seeing his first book in print could reconcile this incorrigible hypochondriac to the dullness of his life in Brittany, or, as he sometimes preferred to think, to the emptiness of existence in general. A visit to Cherbourg only saddens him by recalling a friend, Jean, with whom he has quarrelled. But he does react to the spring. Two mistresses help him to pass the time. In June he is positively joyous. "Never since childhood have I felt so keenly the physical sensation of spring, the renewal of all that lives, the revival of the eternal forces of nature, Life is still beautiful—health and youth are the only real good in this world."

He assumed his favourite disguise as an ordinary sailor, and goes brawling and rollicking about the port.

Friendship, except with people like Yves, he does not believe in. What he wanted was a new *grande passion;* and this he was to find soon after leaving the detested Lorient in June, 1878.

In a letter dated Rochefort, July 15th, he breaks out: "All, all my past life is swept away by a sudden storm, by a passion, an intoxication of the senses against which I am powerless."

He has met a woman of incomparable, inconceivable beauty, who has given herself to him "while loving another, because she loves him (Loti) better." Put more precisely, the woman was the kept mistress of some other man. Loving her, he realises that he has never really loved before.

Shades of Aziyade and the mysterious lady of Geneva! . . .

This passion blazes throughout the summer of 1878. Its scene was the neighbourhood of a great southern seaport. This place, I take to be Bordeaux, since it was visited on fête days by Basques and Béarnais, and was not, apparently, very far from Rochefort. Here he gets in the way of a roystering gang of seamen, old companions in mischief, headed by Gunner Baraba. It is creditable to this man of countless intrigues that he studiously avoids giving any clue to the identity of his mistresses. For this one, he is at pains how to express his love. He becomes extravagant, incoherent, at moments almost grotesque. He hopes they may die together and that in putrefaction their bodies may mingle! Assuredly the nastiest idea that ever emanated from the fevered brain of a lover. He loves "her corruption, her shamelessness, which is a noble and sublime shamelessness like that of an antique Venus." Lower down, he corrects himself. She is not corrupt. It is but the ebullience of her adorable youth. Loved by so many men, she is keenly conscious of the charms of her body and delights in its power. In other words, she was an artist at that sort of thing.

His friend, Plunket, stands astonished before these ecstasies of superb animalism. But very soon the woman tired and returned to her old love. She had given herself to Loti, he says in extenuation, with a fine smile which meant, "Since for what I am worth you love me so much, since positively you must have me—here, take your will of me!"

It was all over by the autumn. Starving for his latest mistress, the unhappy man remembered that only a year before he had been yearning for Aziyade. "My heart," he confessed, "is as changeable as an equinoctial sky."

He had begun to know himself. That acquaintance is generally disagreeable. Till this moment, he had, after the manner of lovers, managed every time he fell in love to persuade himself that on previous occasions he had been mistaken or had loved quite differently. Now, in his twenty-ninth year, he had to realise that he simply had to love. His various mistresses were merely personifications of the other sex. Or, as he might have preferred to put it, his heart was an instrument from which any woman might extract a melody according to her skill.

Most of us have discovered in a painful moment that the "love of our life" was only one of our loves or potential loves. And the man who suffers, no matter how acutely, from repeated attacks of this painful fever, usually gets scant sympathy. I do not know why. You would not refuse your pity to one afflicted with malaria or lumbago or bankruptcy on the ground that he had had attacks just as violent before. For obviously, a previous experience of the agonies in store for him must surely aggravate the victim's misery. I have actually heard a lover moan, "Why did I ever let myself love her like this? —I have been through it all before and know the hell which awaits me." Yet, illogically enough, the favourite hero of romance, the one who gets all the kind words, is the fellow who was disappointed in love once and has never got it again.

Loti, for one, will not renew his claim on our sympathy on this score. We are to hear no more of furious, volcanic loves. It may be that he had learnt his lesson or had overdrawn his passional capacity. It is my belief, however, that as his new interests in life developed, so the importance of passion declined. Women, indeed, continue to be a necessity, the supreme pleasure and reward. But no one woman, so far as I have been able to discover, is again indispensable to him.

On his new ship, the *Moselle*, cruising between the Atlantic ports of France, he soothed his convalescence by thoughts of Senegal, Geneva, and Constantinople. At Cherbourg he renewed his relations with a woman already known to him, and was surprised to find that he almost loved her. But she quickly disappeared. The life of a French naval officer on the home station is so monotonous that the coldest of men might be forgiven such distractions. Meanwhile, Loti was passing the proofs of his first book. He had already begun the second.

CHAPTER IX

FAME AND FORTUNE

"*Aziyade*, being extracts from the notes and letters of an English naval officer in the Turkish service, killed before Kars, 27th October, 1877"—such was the title of Julien Viaud's first published book. With a shyness characteristic of him in early life, he did not let it appear over his signature. It was published by Calmann-Levy in January, 1879.

The author did not leap into fame. Apart from flattering advance notices circulated by the publishers, the only review of importance was Maxime Gaucher's in the *Revue Bleue*. It was by no means eulogistic. The critic finds the author's inventions and affectations irritating to the last degree, but he ends by admitting that the anonymous novel displays talent, style, and wit, and abounds in vivid descriptions and sharply-defined silhouettes.

The reviewer introduces the book by observing that it has made a little noise. Probably, the author's friends in Paris, who were pretty numerous by this time, had contrived to get it and the author talked about. For within a month or two of the publication, Loti had become in a small way a personage. On leave in Paris, he pays a visit to no less a celebrity than Sarah Bernhardt. The great actress had become "she". Writing on May 26th, 1879, he says that she has captured his imagination.* In the uniform of an A.B., one of his favourite disguises, he sits in a stall at the Théatre-Français and sees her act in "Hernani." She gives him a smile of recognition, which—oh, joy of joys!—is remarked by the audience. They direct glances of curiosity and envy at the young sailor.

Our rising author did not, however, get much encouragement from Sarah, who omits even to mention him in her memoirs. Loti was unused to rebuffs, and might, perhaps, have given up the European woman for good had he not just then established some sort of intimacy with a Madame M.R. . . . a widow, certainly, and a *femme de monde*, apparently. He had become acquainted with her, I gather, through his cousins in Paris. At least, she was known to his family in Rochefort, to whom he felt obliged to write some time later, emphatically contradicting a rumour that he was about to marry her. But their intimacy was to last some time. They meet again at Bretenoux, that old haunt of his boyhood, in the following autumn, and

* My friend, Arthur Lynch, who knew most of the literary lights of Paris in Loti's day, is responsible for the following story. "Pierre Loti conceived a great admiration for Sarah Bernhardt, but the feeling was not returned. It was in vain that friends interceded on behalf of the novelist—Sarah would not receive him. One day, however, she received news that an unknown admirer was sending her a beautiful Persian carpet. Her curiosity was aroused. Sure enough the carpet arrived, and Sarah ordered that it should be brought to the drawing-room and shown forthwith. Out of the carpet rolled Pierre Loti! He smiled, bowed, and with a look at once timid and audacious, won the great lady's sympathy. She invited him to stay and they became friends." I am bound to add that I can find no confirmation of this story in Loti's diary.—E.B. d'A.

drive through the pleasant, southern country. Loti always melted under the fire of fine eyes. "If I wasn't absolutely sure that she would forget me within a fortnight," he confesses, "I should reproach myself for this evening's work."

He calls her Marthe and corresponds with her, but with an ill grace. He knows himself well by this time, and frankly warns her not to expect real love, still less physical fidelity, from him. He even gives good advice, recommending her to take a husband rather than a lover; admitting, with a wry smile, that the rôle of moralist does not fit him very well.

By this time he had finished his Tahitian idyll, which was also accepted by Calmann-Levy. The publishers, took care to reserve an option on his work for the next ten years. The book was at first entitled *Rarahu*, and was dedicated to Sarah Bernhardt, a person certainly very unlike the heroine. Whether the great actress thanked the author for the compliment, I do not know; but the work was the means of procuring for Loti the most precious and the most useful of all his friendships.

That great journalist, Juliette Adam, the apostle of the *revanche*, had founded her fortnightly, the *Nouvelle Revue*, on December 1st, 1879. In search of a serial novel, she called upon Calmann-Levy, who showed her a manuscript, the work, they said, of a young naval officer, unknown, but full of promise. "But," claims Mme. Adam, "I alone was the first to perceive that here was a genius of the first order." She wrote to Alexandre Dumas, *fils*, to Alphonse Daudet, and other eminent writers, calling their attention to the story, which appeared in the issues of January and February, 1880, under the title (suggested by the editress), *The Marriage of Loti.* The success, she tells us, was colossal. She doubled the price which the author had accepted for the serial rights.

The romance was immediately after issued in book form by the publishers, as the work of "*the Author of Aziyade.*" No doubt, Rarahu's fairy godmother, Juliette Adam, had smoothed the path; but the enthusiasm of the critics was as genuine as it was eloquent. The *Figaro* declared this to be one of the most captivating books which had appeared for a long time. "What strikes me most," continues the reviewer, "is the note of sincerity in every word of the book. The emotion comes of itself, and the charm is the more powerful, because it is unconscious." Edmond Scherer, writing in the *Temps*, warns the intending reader that the book is hardly a romance, but that it is charming, novel without extravagance, original without effort. A discordant note was struck by Maxime Gaucher. He had not liked *Aziyade,* and he thinks now that the author might have devoted his talents to something better than the recital of unpleasant and vulgar amours.

The author found, at any rate, that he had employed those talents very profitably. Calling at his publishers within three weeks of the book's appearance he drew a thousand francs more than he had expected on account of royalties. The money rolled in so fast that on May 13th, 1880, he was able to discharge the last of the debts which had weighed on his family. Such a success dispelled even the thick fog of gloom with which he loved to envelope himself. He declares it is good to be alive. Free from debt! He asks a shipmate to repeat those words to him every morning. By his sturdy, uncompromising honesty and frankly bourgeois delight in his solvency, Loti reminds us of another great man of letters, in other respects totally dissimilar—Walter Scott.

Sub-lieutenant Viaud's head was not turned by success. Alphonse Daudet and Octave Feuillet expressed a wish to meet him. Fame as well as fortune was knocking at his door; but he preferred to wait a while before lifting the veil of anonymity which covered him. Many a young Englishman, upon so promising a start, would have thrown up his profession and devoted himself entirely to his new career. Such an idea, it is safe to say, never entered our author's head. He shows up very well at this moment. Having saved the honour of his family, he is next anxious to promote the interests of his humble, but much-loved friend, Pierre le Cor— "Frère Yves." He writes to Mme. Adam, pestering her to use her good offices on the man's behalf to obtain him promotion to a higher rating.

He dined with Alphonse Daudet, who, in a letter dated June 2nd, 1880, advises him to stick to nature and poetic writing, and not to trouble about "the story." Though honoured and flattered by the great writer's friendship, Loti was even more interested in his other new friend, Juliette Adam, a widow five years his senior. The acquaintance developed into a warm affection which was to unite them all his life. "I was his second mother," she tells us proudly, though she would have thrust from her the love justly due to the first. She might fairly claim, not only to have discovered Loti's genius, but to have given it, here and there, an inconspicuous, but vital, direction.

Embarking aboard the *Friedland* (April 1st, 1880), the young man must have felt that he was a much more important person than the braid on his cuff implied. But he found time to write long letters to "Marthe" (Mme. M.R.) and informed her, among other things, that he had bought a little jackal, which slept on his chest at night and, on catching sight of the moon, would brace its fore-paws against his body and howl. It was the howl which had often kept Loti awake in the Senegal country—perhaps he found it usefully reminiscent at this stage. At Algerian ports he talked to the Muslims about the capital of the Caliphate, and had produced for his delectation an aged Turk, a survivor of the Ottoman vassalage. At Algiers (the French) Jack Ashore supplied the incidents for his short story, *Les Trois Dames de la Kasbah.*

Returning to Toulon, he parted with the jackal, (*une brave pétite bête*), whom he handed over to a friendly circus proprietor. At a *hotel garni*, which he calls the Capharnaum, he settled down to hard work, resolutely closing his door against jolly good fellows, and equally jolly nice girls. On June 1st he began *The Romance of a Spahi*, finishing it by the end of the month—assuredly a fine performance. Writing to

Daudet on the 10th, he says: "It is a more painful and lengthy business than I had reckoned on, my *Spahi*. It is fatiguing to furbish up my memories of sun and sand, still more to recall personal adventures which meant a good deal of suffering for me." Later, in his diary, he says: "I pass these lovely June days writing—exhuming my memories of the Senegal, in order to make money out of them."

Daudet, it is interesting to note, when he had seen the completed manuscript, strongly urged Loti to leave out the sentimental passages about the "dear girl in France," and all the letters from mother. Make France as far away as possible, something low down beyond the horizon, was the gist of the elder man's advice. It was not followed, or at least only partially, as we know, by Loti.

On June 22nd, 1880, the *Friedland* left the neighbourhood of Toulon, and, in the first week of July, Loti found himself at Rochefort. His great-aunt, Lalie, one of his dear old people, had died in his absence. His African romance finished, he was now meditating a story of Brittany. The *Friedland* took him on to Cherbourg and Brest. He visited Rosporden, and made an intensive study of the life of the country folk. On August 10th, the fleet was reviewed by President Grévy. Loti's utter want of interest in the chief magistrate of the republic contrasts with his childish and most un-French enthusiasm for kings and queens—especially queens.

In September, the *Friedland* was ordered to the Adriatic. Various Powers had sent their ships there to see what was doing in Montenegro and

Albania. Loti remained in these parts till the end of November. He visited Ragusa, Cattaro, and Gravosa, and made excursions up country into Hercegovina and Montenegro. He has left us some fine descriptions of this rugged coast—he speaks of the "lunar desolation" of the highlands; but Europe, outside his own country, seems to have stirred his imagination very little. Half the charm of the European scene usually lies in its associations, suggested or manifest; and Loti knew as little about the history and legends of southern Europe as does the cheaper sort of American tourist.

In the Montenegrins, however, he recognised the traditional foes of the Turks. The Austrian officers he got on very well with; but he felt, as always, that you cannot know a country till you know its women in the biblical sense. Behind a coast village, he scraped acquaintance with a Hercegovinian girl employed in tending sheep and goats. She smelt, he admits, not only of the new-mown hay, but also of the cowshed and the sheep which she guarded. But at night he was conscious only of the beauty of her body and the simplicity of her mind. He could not, of course, speak her language, but that was an obstacle which he was accustomed to disregard. Perhaps, without being aware of it, he had become more fastidious in his thirty-first year. It is certain that he has not succeeded in making Pasquala Ivanovitch as sympathetic a figure as the Tahitian savage or the Circassian odalisque.

The year 1881 opens well for Loti, with his promotion to lieutenant. Back in home waters, he started a correspondence with Emile Pouvillion, a novelist whose works greatly attracted him. But it was not till the autumn that he would consent to meet this friend in the flesh at his home at Montauban. He was ever difficult and finicky in his friendships with men, dreading disillusionment, and believing, or affecting to believe, that affection must necessarily languish as acquaintance became closer. A good many literary people prefer the friend at a distance to the friend next door, because they can express their own individualities to their hearts' content in letters, and need not read the replies. They hope, too, that you are preserving their letters with a view to publication. I remember one man who never forgave me for having torn up a few lines which he had written me from Italy; and another— a Californian poet—who admitted frankly that he wanted, not so much a friend as a correspondent.

By this time, it had dawned on the naval authorities that, under the modest description of Lieutenant Viaud, there existed in the service a personage of importance to the world at large. The admiral, Loti tells us, with a friendly smile congratulated him upon his last book. Being a Frenchman, and having, therefore, a real respect for letters, the admiral probably meant it. The officer in our services who earns literary or artistic distinction, it may be remarked, in generally regarded by his superiors and comrades as more an oddity than a celebrity. Actors, it need hardly be said, are on a very different footing, and were regarded during the late war, even by the real, regular, Sandhurst-

PIERRE LOTI AS A NAVAL LIEUTENANT.

bred colonel, with a very genuine interest and esteem.

For the time being Loti settled down as secretary at naval headquarters at his native town. His third romance appeared under the title of *The Spahi* in the *Nouvelle Revue* in the spring of '81, to be published as *The Romance of a Spahi* in the autumn. This time, the author signed himself Pierre Loti, and allowed his identity to be established. The *Figaro* announced that Pierre Loti was the pseudonym of a distinguished sailor, M. Julien Viaud, first-lieutenant in the navy, who not only wrote charming romances, but was an accomplished musician, much appreciated at Rochefort. M. Viaud, moreover, was understood to be no inconsiderable artist, and his drawings had been received with favour by the public.

Remembering his injuries at the hands of the engraver, the fortunate author must have winced at this last piece of flattery. But he must have relished the favourable reviews which attended his last book. He had become known by his works to the members of the "Parisian gallantry" to whom he was presented in October. They had all read his books—or said so. Under the same date—almost the last in his diary as so far published—he records a charming evening with Mme. Adam, who tried to convert him to her own obscure and heterodox theory of death and a future life.

They were still exchanging views on this solemn topic, the following April. To the author of *Paienne*, Loti writes: "That faith, that ideal of which you speak, I have it not, and I only half understand it; but from you I will accept it. In my childhood, I had a deep faith, a passionate attachment to Christ. Since then, I have passed through many phases. At present, my state of mind is a vague, dismal pantheism. Above all I love the sun, the lonely places in the woods, where I can rest and forget everything. I understand nature in a manner at once profound, mysterious, and uncanny. I lose myself in her.

"With that goes a horror of all progress, modern ideas and things, social obligation, solidarity, etc. And a cult of souvenir for all the past.

"My life goes in fighting the fragility of things, in an effort to keep hold of the things that pass, and to recover the dead past.

"And then, I think with supreme terror of the moment when old age will come, and I shall no more be loved."

He rejects Juliette's god, Apollo, and prefers Baal Zebub, the god of corruption. Paradoxically enough, he is dismayed at finding his friend also to be a pagan, wishing she could draw him towards Christianity.

With Loti, unhappily, we have learnt to be on the look-out for pose; but here he speaks sincerely enough. No man more genuinely wanted to believe —in a personal God and in a hereafter. Death was not for him a sleep, but a horror. As he grew older he reached out more eagerly than before towards something beyond—and grasped nothing.

Within a very few weeks of writing this letter, it looked as though he might have an early opportunity of solving these terrific problems by personal experience. War had broken out in France's far eastern sphere of influence. The province of Tongking had transferred its allegiance from France to China, and a formidable body of irregulars, called the Black Flags, threatened resistance to the white barbarians. The natives were in the right, as they generally have been in their troubles with the rapacious and piratical western powers. Tongking, and the whole empire of Annam, of which it was a province, were old and willing feudatories of the Middle Kingdom. The government of Jules Ferry, having made itself very unpopular in France was, of course, glad of the war as a means of distracting attention from affairs at home. Loti was ordered to embark on the *Atalante*, under orders for the East.

It does not appear that he rejoiced at the prospect of seeing active service for the first time. Fragments of his diary, which in some mysterious manner found their way into the possession of Lafcadio Hearn and were translated by him, apprize us that Loti, on the eve of his departure, plunged into yet another "love" affair at Brest, hoping that it might enable him to forget the other—the true one—which the campaign interrupted. At this one can only smile wearily and ask, which, or what, love was this, in Cupid's name?

The *Atalante*, on which our author was only an officer passenger, sailed on May 29th, 1883. The record of the voyage is to be found in *Propos d'exil*, and the translated diary just mentioned. The latter,

I cannot help thinking, was touched up or originally intended for publication, for it contains no less improbable an incident than Loti's discovering on board, in his actual watch, an Arab fireman who had known him and Aziyade at Constantinople! But we have no difficulty in believing that, in its course, the warship passed over the very place where the body of Loti's brother had been committed to the deep, twenty years before. A little while later, the author was knocked over by sunstroke. He relapsed into insensibility and speechlessness, while retaining, he tells us, complete mental lucidity and consciousness of approaching death. "All my past appeared before me, incredibly, awfully remote. The great pain was the thought that I should never see my mother again. But next I thought with a kind of strange gladness that all the errors and torments of life were about to pass away for ever in one great irrevocable blotting-out, and that the eternal peace was coming. . . .

"And then, all of a sudden, my arms relaxed, my clenched fingers unbent, and speech returned to me. . . . I was saved.

"And yet I had been so calm in that dream of nothingness. I had traversed the moment of the last agony. Why have recalled me, I thought, to passions, to regrets, to the great struggle of life? Why, seeing that some day I must reach that awful moment. . . . ?"*

* This passage, translated from a great French stylist by a great English stylist, makes one of the worst pieces of English I have ever read. I have ventured slightly to amend it. E.B. d'A.

CHAPTER X

AN INDISCREET OFFICER

REFERENCE was made just now to the superior esteem in which the actor, as officer, was held in our British services. The estimate might be justified on these grounds. The actor is trained to say and do what he is told; the author's business is to say what he thinks. We now find Loti, the author, on his first experience of active service, very nearly ruining Julien Viaud, naval lieutenant.

The *Atalante* sighted the coast of Annam at the moment Admiral Courbet, the French Commander-in-Chief, had resolved to teach the monarch of that country a severe lesson. Loti, in his capacity of passenger, witnessed, from the deck of the *Atalante*, the bombardment and taking of the forts of Thuan-An, which defended the approach to the capital, Hué. He took no part in the action. But the spectacle was one which no literary man could waste. Supplementing his own observations by the communications of a friend, Lieut. Poidloue, who had been in charge of a landing party, he committed his impressions to writing and sent them to the Paris *Figaro*.

His articles appeared in the issues of September 28th, October 13th, and October 17th, 1883. The two first were introduced as the work of an officer on the spot who had necessarily to remain anonymous; the third was announced as from the pen of Pierre Loti, the distinguished author of *Mariage de Loti*, etc., and of a new novel entitled *Mon Frère Yves*, (which had already appeared in the *Revue des Deux Mondes*), to be published forthwith by Calmann-Lévy. I presume that eminent publishing house will not, at this late date, repudiate responsibility for the concluding intimation.

The editor of the *Figaro* was certainly right in calling these articles not only an important historical document, but a fine piece of literature. It was as vivid and realistic a performance as any that Loti ever achieved. Dread of his own extinction had never extinguished in him a taste for the macabre, as readers of the *Spahi* will remember; and that taste he fully indulged in the following remarkable passages:

"Our sailors run across the sandhills, surprise the Annamites before they have time to seize their arms, and smash them with the butts of their rifles, as if the thing were a game. A thousand men, perhaps, flee before a handful of bluejackets."

Much worse is to come:

"The French, mounting the walls of the fort, fire down upon the enemy almost point-blank, and kill them *en masse*. The Annamites drop in batches, arms outstretched. Three or four hundred are mown down in less than five minutes by quick fire and volleys. Touched with pity, the sailors cease firing and let the remainder escape."

Elsewhere—"The rifles had been sighted for the correct distance, magazines were charged. Our men were ready for the fugitives. They issued in groups, half scorched, from their village. Hesitating, they girded up their loins to run, protecting their heads against our bullets with planks, mats, and baskets—such precautions as one might take against a shower of rain! Then they made a dash for it. The battle began. We let them have two volleys—one, two! It was curious to see these waves of bullets, two a minute, overwhelm them so surely and methodically, at the word of command.

"Some picked themselves up and started to run frantically, like wounded beasts. They ran the death-race in zigzags, in all directions, round and round. Their top-knots went loose, and their long hair flew about, giving them the appearance of women.

"Others threw themselves into the lagoon, covering their heads with matting, and tried to reach the junks. They were killed as they swam. Some dived under water, and remained under a long while; but they were caught when, like seals, they rose to the surface for a mouthful of air.

"Our people amused themselves by counting the dead. Fifty to the left, eighty to the right. In the village they lay in little heaps. Some of them, badly scorched, were not quite dead. Here and there, an arm or leg was thrust out stiff, in someone's final agony, or a shriek was heard.

" Then the sailors of the fort, maddened by the sun and the noise, hurried out, and in a sort of nervous excitement, threw themselves upon the wounded. There were still Annamites hiding in the holes, shamming dead; they held out their hands for mercy, crying, '*Han, han!*' in a frightful voice. The French finished them with the butts of their rifles."

Officers here and there protested against this massacre of the wounded and defenceless. The men refused to listen, maddened by stories of atrocities perpetrated by the yellow men. "After all," observes the narrator, "in the Far East, these are the usages of war. When, with a small handful of men, you attempt to subjugate an immense country, you must go on killing and spreading terror around you, or perish yourself."

This last defence of "frightfulness" does not ring true. It is perfectly evident that Loti wrote under the liveliest sensations of horror and disgust. And those sensations, intentionally or not, he aroused in his readers. The publication of these articles in the Parisian newspaper came as an unpleasant shock. The *Parlement*, a ministerial organ, quoted by *The Times*, under date Oct. 23rd, 1883, stigmatized the last article as "containing revolting details of the atrocities imputed to our sailors. . . . That sailors, exasperated by Capt. Rivière's death and the more or less imaginative accounts given of it, should have avenged it on Annamite soldiers who had no hand in it, is deplorable—it is to be strongly condemned—but after all, it is intelligible. What is more difficult to conceive is that an officer has been found to make the scene of butchery the subject of a literary sketch. It will not surprise us if the Chinese Government, being notoriously well-informed of what is printed in Europe, should seize on this letter and circulate it in the Extreme East, and if, some day, it should serve as a plea for fearful reprisals."

On which *The Times* quietly comments that the correctness of the account in question does not seem to be disputed.

Henry Rochefort, who was then conducting a furious campaign against the Ferry Government, seized eagerly on the articles. In the *Intransigeant* he asks if it is not appalling that these horrors, recalling the massacres of 1871, of the Communists by the Government troops, should have been perpetrated to satisfy the cupidity of Jules Ferry's financial friends and *chevaliers d'industrie* ? Loti is praised for his magnanimous condemnation of his comrades' barbarity. The Germans got hold of the articles, and made their own comments on French civilisation. I have not been able to trace any specific comments in the English press ; but I suppose we thought a lot.

The answer of the ministry was contained in a circular (Oct. 28th, 1883), calling attention to the regulation under which "it was forbidden to any officer, functionary, or agent of the ministry of marine, to publish anything whatsoever, signed, unsigned, or signed with a pseudonym, without having first obtained the sanction of the minister." At the same time, Admiral Courbet was informed of his subordinate's indiscretion, and called on for an early report.

Loti cried out in alarm and indignation at the storm he had brought about his own head. What grieved and exasperated him most was that his article should have been interpreted as an attack on the French sailor, whom he found so splendid, so fine. . . .* His astonishment may strike us as ingenuous, but it was undoubtedly sincere. His picture was not all red, looked at closely—he had stippled it here and there with tributes to the valour of his comrades, even to their tardy humanity. He describes a sailor, after the bombardment, coming across an Annamite who begged for mercy—the tar wagged his finger at him as at a child and said: "Mercy, certainly, but you must carry my barrel for me." In another place, we are told, the sailors, having expended their fury, busied themselves with searching and caring for the enemy wounded. He resorts even to the ignominious excuse of panic— the panic of young Breton fisherboys confronted with a hideous yellow foe in whom they had been taught to recognise the devil himself.

But the purple patches were so large as almost to cover the canvas. Loti, the humanest of men, no doubt, regarded the frightfulness he had witnessed as inseparable from war. He meant no reproach to the men who waged it. But his descriptive genius carried his sentiments along with it. He wrote at once to the *Figaro*, protesting against the point of view attributed to him. That letter was never

* Letter to Mme. Adam, Dec. 9th, 1883, from Touran.

published, M. Serban thinks it was suppressed by Government order.

To Juliette Adam, he wrote: "I am sacrificed to please the English and the Germans." (What in the world had the English to do with it? One is reminded of the twaddle about the Hidden Hand that made our press ridiculous in the last war). "I've asked Alphonse Daudet to express my indignation to the public, to the journalists. Let them know, at least, how much I love these *savage* sailors, how much I belong to them, how I am on their side! If I am forced to quit the service it will be a knock-down blow. I love my profession, and seafaring folk above all others. I want to stick with them, no matter what indignities I am made to submit to."

He must have been devoted to his profession, since he did not contemplate sending in his papers, as many a man sure of a brilliant career outside the service would have been tempted to do. He passed an anxious two months in the bay of Touran, close to Hué, interesting himself in the little yellow people, and collecting souvenirs. At last, on December 14th, he writes, "I have received, by a passing steamer, a very unexpected order of recall to Paris. The *Corrèze* is the transport that will take me back to France. I leave to-morrow! Things in the navy are always done at a moment's notice."

He had been hoping, I suppose, that the whole affair had blown over. The recall came as a very painful shock. "Night," he continues, "finds me ready. Ready to follow my destiny, and to say good-bye to the companions of my exile. I turned in late, agitated by this upset in my life.

"There remains nothing for me to do. I have 'handed over', and my trunks are packed. I cannot recall another departure so calm." But the transport did not appear that day. At sundown he surveyed the mountains of Annam a little wistfully. "Odd, how one ends by attaching oneself to everything." Yes, even to a dug-out in a muddy trench, or a corrugated-iron shed somewhere behind the line. Isn't it Byron who remarks:

" Even on leaving the most unpleasant places and
        people,
    Somehow one keeps on looking at the steeple?"

The *Corrèze* arrives in the night. "Well, it really is good-bye, this time. This chapter of my life is closed." Next morning he sailed. "Officers and men wave to me with their caps. I feel myself on the verge of tears when all that disappears—when the familiar mountains close in on the bay of Touran, when the tops of the *Circe* go down out of sight.

"Before mid-day we are out of sight of land. There succeeds that calm of the ocean which effaces everything. The *Circe* and the bay of Touran are obliterated, leaving hardly a memory behind.

"I knew that would be so, but hardly so soon. Well, well! it is only love that has ever been able to attach me more or less lastingly to the strange places of the earth."*

* *Propos d'Exil.*

The lump in his throat may have gone, but one can see that his heart was still heavy. Disgrace he believed, awaited him.

But he became interested in the ship, which was conveying a number of sick. His impressions he afterwards embodied in one of the most moving and vivid passages of *Pêcheur d'Islande*. At Singapore, he went ashore for three hours. It may have been on this trip or the next that he visited the forlorn little Indian colony of Mahé, where the tricolour floats over a *mairie*, and, at moments, one might take oneself to be in a town of southern France. Loti tells a story about the inhabitants which I cannot help reproducing here. An Indian of Mahé being cited before a Corsican magistrate in Indo-China, and being treated by him as though he were "a native," indignantly burst out, "I am a Frenchman. We were French at Mahé two hundred years before you were!"

In the meantime, Lieutenant Viaud's fate was being settled in the Rue Royale. Admiral Courbet had ordered his chief-of-staff to reply to the Minister of Marine. The report was contemptuous. Lieut. Viaud had not taken part in the action of Thuan-An; his article had been founded on the gossip of the wardroom, and on the statements of Lieut. Poidloue, with regard to whom suitable action had been taken. The report suggested that the article had been published in order to advertise Lieut. Viaud's forthcoming novel.

On the strength of this report, Loti was placed on half-pay. But powerful influence was brought to bear in his favour. The author had made many friends by this time in the salons of Paris, and the cabinet of Jules Ferry was not, perhaps, unwilling to reduce its unpopularity in aristocratic circles. Juliette Adam had, of course, been at work. "I pleaded his cause and won it," she says. So when Loti, white-faced and anxious, arrived at Toulon, he learnt that he had merely been placed on the supernumerary list.

He got off, some may think, rather lightly. Imagine, if you please, the fate of a British naval officer who, while on active service, wrote to the London papers describing acts of barbarism committed by British sailors! It was a dangerous thing, we know, during the last war to suggest that the Germans were not quite so black as they were painted. If you had any friends at court, the least that you could expect was to be certified by a kindly medical board as more or less mentally deranged.

CHAPTER XI

LOTI remained on shore for the next thirteen months (February, 1884, to March, 1885). He scowled back at the cloud under which he languished. "I cannot help holding it in contempt and hatred, this republic, the offspring of the Philistines! I hope the blood of our sailors will fall on the heads of our rulers." In such terms Lieutenant Viaud, of the French navy, expressed his feelings towards the Government of France. These sentiments, it may be remarked, were merely the outcome of his personal resentment. He never had decided any political opinions or belonged to any definite political faction. He hated Jules Ferry's Government because it had punished him, and he disapproved of the war in the East, and the colonial policy which resulted, because the war had so nearly been the cause of his disgrace. So we may presume that it did not distress him to be absent from the scene of operations. Indeed not much honour was to be reaped in eastern waters, even when Admiral Courbet, on August 23rd, 1884, attacked and destroyed the Chinese fleet at Foo-Choo before, apparently, the Chinese were aware that the French were at war with them.

Loti wrote very little this year, possibly because he now had to ask leave to publish anything. One of his articles, *Un Vieux*, first published at the end of the year in the *Revue des Deux Mondes*, owes much of its sombre hue to the writer's quarrel with existence.

In a letter to Juliette Adam, he laments his lack of physical beauty—a queer complaint to come from a naval officer thirty-four years of age! "Alas! I, too, perhaps would have been handsome if I had had another sort of physical training. I was reared like a hot-house plant. Afterwards, when I grew up, I tried to refashion my body upon the Grecian model by means of physical exercises, but it was too late to acquire all the strength that lacked, or to change my faded countenance. I would give the whole world for the good looks which I lack!"

Most men of his age have got pretty well used to their looks. Nor can I agree that he had been hardly dealt with in this matter. He was not tall, it is true, and his forehead receded. It is certain that no early training would have corrected that defect. Women, at any rate, pretty generally found him attractive, and their favour at all times made the sun and fine weather for him.

Mme. Adam's friendship meant much to him at this stage. "I pressed my lips," he writes (May 19th), "to where, in your letter of this morning, you call me 'son'. But, with my habitual dread of the fragility of all things, I fear that before long this may pass, that you will care for me no longer, having seen too much of me."

He need not have feared. Juliette Adam loved him to the day of his death—and beyond. To her, also, he was indebted for his life-long friendship with Jean Aicard. The two writers were about the same age: Mme. Adam used to speak of them as her two sons. Some of Loti's happiest hours were spent at Aicard's house, in an arid part of Provence. It was a warm friendship at first between two men rather than between two authors, observes one who knew both,* but, in the long run, it became a literary friendship also. We find Loti writing from the deck of the *Formidable,* in June, 1891, asking his friend's opinion on certain passages in his *Livre de la Pitié et de la Mort.* Years after, he had the great happiness of securing Aicard's election to the Academy, and pronouncing the address of welcome. The two friends were not long separated in the end. Jean Aicard died within a year or two of his friend.

Briefer was Loti's acquaintance with another literary lady, Mrs. Lee Childe, a Frenchwoman, I gather, who had married an American. To her memory he dedicated his *Propos d'exil,* published in 1887. But by now his friends of both sexes were legion. He knew dukes and duchesses, all the leaders of Parisian society, and was honoured as English society honours famous actresses and fashionable portrait painters. In France, authors are genuinely regarded as persons of very real importance, even when they have nothing to say about religious,

* *Revue Bleue,* July 29th, 1923.

moral, or economic problems. Loti was primarily valued as a great man of letters, but his amazingly frank revelations of his passions and emotions must have excited curiosity as to the man. Invitations to meet Pierre Loti were often welcomed, I suspect, as invitations to meet the lover of Aziyade and Rarahu.

In his latest book, *Mon Frère Yves*, he appeared as the friend, not as the lover. The hero of the story was the sailor, Pierre le Cor, on whose behalf he was for ever asking people to use their influence. Here was proof that Loti's charm did not depend on an exotic atmosphere, nor on purely amorous confessions. He could interest when talking about other people than himself. The whole book, moreover, breathed his love for the French sailor and the stock from which he sprang. It undid, therefore, any harm that might have been done the author in public estimation by the indiscreet articles in the *Figaro*. Not that the harm had been great—the war in the East appears to have been looked on more as Jules Ferry's affair than France's. Loti, in his enforced retirement at Rochefort, should have been soothed by the reception of his first novel of Breton life. What the actual hero felt, we are not told. Frère Yves was just then on active service in Tunis, and, in a very brief note to his friend and patron, announced with seamanlike terseness: "We have just taken the town of Sfax."

The risks his friend of the lower deck was then running, his haunting sense of the "frailty of all human relationships," urged the successful author "to run his desperate bark upon the rocks," in Stevenson's delightful phrase. For the first time he speaks seriously of marrying and settling down. He goes about the matter in the business-like manner of his nation. To Juliette Adam, he writes, "I should like to marry and that soon, before I am sent back to that hell of a China. If I am sent, I shall not return, or when I do, my youth will have fled.

"I seek a girl, simple as I am complex, moderately pretty, and of a sound constitution. Protestant, if possible, because of our family traditions, and with a little money, for I have none.

"If, upon your path, you come across this rare bird, you must let me know."

Apparently, Mme. Adam knew no such young person. Loti was to remain a bachelor some time longer. In the meantime, "that hell of a China" loomed nearer. The ministry were clearly of opinion that Lieut. Viaud had done penance long enough, and might be more usefully employed. In March, 1885, Loti talks about being "torn between the desire to go to Tongking and the desire to go to Iceland." I do not think Tongking attracted him very powerfully. In fact, he asked Mme. Adam to get him sent north. Still, he did not wish it to be supposed that he was shirking. To do him justice, it should be said that his mother, poor old lady, now in her 76th year, was appalled at the possibility of losing her only surviving son in those waters where his brother had perished. Urged by her, he presented himself before the admiral with the intention of asking to be put on the Iceland list. Instead of which, so he tells his friend, he found himself asking to be sent to the East at once. On leaving the admiral's office, he was handed a note. It was from his mother, withdrawing her entreaties, and declaring that in this matter she resigned herself to the dispositions of Providence. Loti embarked at Toulon on the transport Mytho and sailed for the seat of war on March 20th, 1885.

Upon his arrival in Chinese waters (May 5th, 1885) he reported for duty on the ironclad, *Triomphante*, then in the roads of Makung. He received a cordial welcome from the admiral and his former shipmates. The inglorious war had entered on a new and stagnant phase; the French were blockading the mouth of the Yang-tse-Kiang, and had occupied the insignificant Pescadores Islands. Loti was to assist at no event of historical interest except the death of his commander. In the ship's log he records in his own neat, small handwriting, under date June 11th, "At 9.45, Vice-Admiral Courbet, commander-in-chief, died aboard the *Bayard*."

His impressions of this event were given in an article contributed to the *Revue des Deux Mondes* (afterwards included in the volume *Propos d'exil*). Courbet had not proved himself a great admiral, but it was natural that the French, who had had no naval successes for over a century, should esteem him such. "His glory," writes Loti, "is known all over the world. I shall not speak of it here"; and he goes on to speak of his dead chief's consideration for his men, and many seamanlike virtues. (There had been a mutiny on his fleet, though, and a dozen mutineers had been shot). "Only five or six days before," went on our author, "he came on board our ship to witness the launching of our torpedoes, and I remember his shaking hands with me with a simple and exquisite kindness." Of that kindness the lieutenant, still smarting under his late reproof, was deeply sensible, and expressed his gratitude very nobly. The admiral had no doubt been impressed by the favourable report rendered by Loti's former commander, the captain of the *Atalante*.

A few days later peace was proclaimed. Within a month the islands were evacuated by the French. Aboard the *Triomphante*, Loti had the cheery companionship of Frère Yves, now a sort of petty officer. To the Breton sailor he owed a good deal during the composition of *Pêcheur d'Islande*, which he had now begun. He did not work easily at first in the China seas in full summer. The weather was increasingly hot, oppressive and thunderous. "To work better," he tells Mme. Adam, "I concentrate my thoughts on *Her* whom I love always, she who came from Gaud's country." Two months later: "I will send you my romance in three parts. I have never been so undecided about any of my works. One day, I am quite satisfied, the next hopelessly discouraged. I have completely recast the story. After a long mental debate, I have decided to change the girl, who, as you know, was a portrait. At the same time, I suppressed the scenes which it was painful for me to describe, and in which I had been to blame. This seems better to me—it makes for unity. And then on *her* account, my conscience is easier. I am very anxious about the verdict of the public. I wish you were here to advise me on one or two points, though I seldom listen to anyone. And if I can't correct the proofs myself, I should like to be sure that they will be revised by you, in whom alone I have confidence."

It is fortunate that he decided to recast the story. Otherwise it could not have been at all like the masterpiece it is; for in all the long gallery of women whom, so far, we know Loti to have loved, we fail to find one in any way resembling Gaud! He may have been thinking of a girl from Tréguier, to whose influence upon his imagination, about his twenty-seventh year, he partly attributes his sympathy with Brittany. This he says in the *Roman d'un Enfant*, but I find no mention of such a girl in his diary of the years referred to. In writing thus to Mme. Adam, he was magnifying some passing fancy into another "love of his life." Even when talking about his literary work, Loti could not resist the temptation to dramatize himself.

It is worthy of note that he thought at first of calling the book *Au Large* (The Open Sea), but sent his correspondent a list of alternative titles. He also asked her to send his mother any monies due to him from the *Nouvelle Revue*.

CHAPTER XII

A JAPANESE MARRIAGE

THE letter last quoted is dated from Kobe, September 26th, 1885. Upon the conclusion of hostilities, and the evacuation of the Pescadores, the *Triomphante* had proceeded to Japanese waters. In the interval had occurred Loti's headlong plunge into Japanese life, which is the narrative of *Madame Chrysanthème*. But for that experience, I do not think *Pêcheur d'Islande* would have been as good a book. The author's experience of Japan was not exactly a disillusionment, because he does not seem to have approached that country with any particular enthusiasm; but he emerged from it dissatisfied and chagrined. In that mood his thoughts turned eagerly and lovingly to the very different women of his own western world. His second novel of Brittany was completed, I fancy, under the influence of home-sickness, an ailment now unusual with him.

Loti had been passably bored during the wretched naval operations in the China seas. Within the last sixty years or so war has become a boring business. The old wars not infrequently resembled a duel, or a fight within the ropes; the combatants stood up to each other, and the issue was soon decided. Nowadays we are reminded more of two men, both horribly afraid, watching each other from opposite corners, both frightened to make the next move. Ancient war was a dog fight, modern war is like a cat fight. I half suspect that a good many men desert in modern wars not because they object to fighting, but because they don't get enough of it.

Our sailor had certainly seen death at close hand in the China seas, but it was death by cholera, not by the foeman's steel. The sight of those rough-and-ready burials in enemy soil had powerfully depressed him. From the neighbourhood of death, he turned with a renewed longing towards life. Besides, since he had left Pasquala Ivanovitch, presumably to lament him on the shores of Dalmatia, he had not had a really sustained love affair. In the circumstances, we need not excuse Loti for looking forward to an orgy of the flesh in Japan.

At sea, under a clear starlit sky, on the bridge, he announced his plan to Frère Yves. "As for me, I shall at once marry."

"Ah!" said Yves, with the indifferent air of a man whom nothing can surprise.

"Yes. I shall choose a little yellow-skinned woman with black hair and cat's eyes. She must be pretty. Not much bigger than a doll. You shall have a room in our house. A little paper house, in the midst of green gardens, prettily shaded. We shall live among flowers, everything round us shall blossom, and each morning our dwelling shall be filled with nosegays, such as you have never dreamt of."

The warship cast anchor off Nagasaki on July 8th. The sight of the port quickly dispelled Loti's first, and favourable, impressions of this new country. A crowd of peddlers, boatmen, long-shoremen, swarmed on to the decks. "Lord," exclaims Loti, "how ugly, mean, and grotesque, these people are."

Not encouraging, surely, to one about to marry a Japanese! But urged partly by curiosity, partly by the lusts of the flesh, Loti persevered in his design. He tells us how he landed in drenching rain, and was carried in a rickshaw to the tea-house recommended to him by experienced friends. Step by step, disappointment dogs him. But he gets hold of the man whose name had been given him, and makes him understand that he wants a wife. The foreigner is hard to please. Perhaps he would not have taken a wife at all, if Frère Yves had not called his attention to a girl in dark blue. With more misgivings than he had plunged into amours in Polynesia, Turkey, and Dalmatia, Loti engages the young creature as his wife at a salary of twenty dollars a month. The arrangement was formally ratified at the police-station next day. Loti writes to Juliette Adam to announce that he has tem-porarily married Okane-San—he calls her Mme. Chrysanthème in his book, as we know.

The book is interesting or not in proportion to your interest in Japan. Some of us wouldn't trouble to visit that country, even if it were accessible by a penny 'bus from Charing Cross. To others, like Lafcadio Hearn, it is the land of heart's desire, the wonderful country over the hills. Loti never, at any time, saw Japan through the gorgeous mist of Hearn's imagination, and the bleak reality dawned on him very much sooner. But outside his absurd ménage, he had quite interesting experiences. Among these was a state ball at the Ministry of Foreign Affairs. His account, given in the *Nouvelle Revue* in December, 1887, might have, he thought, a certain historic interest even for the actual inhabitants of a country which has undergone so rapid an evolution. At that time (it may still be so) the Japanese ladies cut a displeasing figure in their Parisian toilettes. Contrasting marvellously with these persons of lower rank, the princesses of the blood, and certain court ladies, made a dramatic entrance in ceremonial attire—a costume "never seen in the street nor in pictures, immemorially prescribed for the court and never seen elsewhere. Trousers of scarlet silk, stiff and flaring, like an enormous crinoline on each leg . . . above this, a garment, like a priest's chasuble, falling without a fold from the neck to the ankles . . . the black hair stretched, drawn, and twisted on some sort of frame, surrounding the little inanimate yellow face like a fan or a peacock's tail. The head, like the body, seems to be all breadth. You might take these for persons escaped from some book in which they had lain flattened and preserved for centuries. Ugly perhaps—and yet I'm not sure—ugly, but supremely distinguished, and possessing a certain

charm. Eyeing the festival somewhat disdain-
fully, with an enigmatical smile in their half-shut
eyes, these ladies seat themselves apart, forming,
in the midst of the ball, a group of mysterious
aspect."

Anything new in the shape of woman made an
irresistible appeal to Loti. We are not surprised to
learn that, contrary, as he had been warned, to
every law of Japanese etiquette, he deliberately
walked over to the group, and asked one of these
impressive beings for a dance. Loti was, as Mr.
Arnold Bennett would say, "a card." He spoke in
French. The lady did not understand him. A
companion rose and, looking at the bold intruder
with bright intelligent eyes, asked him in French,
with "an accent of bizarre distinction," what he
wanted.

"The honour of dancing with her."

"The little black eyebrows shot up—every shade
of surprise was expressed in her look. She bent her
wide frame of a head towards the other and translated the astounding demand."

"Smiles—and their two pairs of eyes were turned
upon me. Very graciously, very prettily, in spite
of my audacity, the one who speaks French thanks
me, and explains that they do not know the modern
dances. This is probably true, but it is not the
only reason. Decorum forbids it absolutely, I am
well aware." It only remains to the bold French
lieutenant to retire, regretting that he cannot continue the conversation with his interpreter, whose
voice and expression he finds charming.

Thus, Japanese court etiquette proved an insurmountable barrier to the curiosity which had o'erleapt harem lattices. The hope which, I doubt not, Loti had for one moment indulged of having a love affair with one of these extraordinary unhuman princesses, faded. It is a pity for us. The adventure would have made a better story than that of his relations with the hired mousmé.

"Neither the heart nor the senses," observes M. Serban, "had any part in this union. In fact, its sole purpose appeared to be to enable Loti to escape from the international life of the hotels, and to penetrate into a genuinely Japanese environment. Absolutely convinced that a European could not fathom a Japanese mind, he renounced right away the experiment, attempted in Oceania and Constantinople, of acquiring for himself a local soul. The impression which Japan left upon him was that of a world radically incompatible with our European sensibility, of a world where all the proportions are false, where the trees are dwarfs, and the flowers giants, where respect for convention and art has stifled all spontaneous sentiment. The only side of Japanese life which seems to have interested him, except the picturesque background, was perhaps this impassibility, this complete mastery or total absence of the sentiments, which implies a life entirely fashioned and governed by pattern and standards."

Paradoxically, Loti, the master of literary style, cared little for art or style. He wanted nature, warm flesh. Whatever he had heard beforehand about Japan must have prepared him for a wholly artificial world. He had no illusions to be shattered, but he liked the place and its people even less than he expected to do.

"After all, I do not positively detest this little Chrysanthemum," he yawns, "and when there is no repugnance on either side, habit turns into a makeshift of attachment. . . . What a pity this little Chrysanthemum cannot always be asleep; she is really extremely decorative seen in this manner— and like this, at least, she does not bore me." He suspects Yves of taking more than a platonic interest in her; and, in all probability, is disappointed upon finding this is not so—a dull woman may achieve a kind of interest when she is deceiving you.

The order to sail must have come as a release. Loti almost hoped that approaching separation might evoke something of tenderness or sentiment. But on the eve of his departure he found her carefully testing the silver dollars he had paid her with! "Well, little mousmé," he writes, "let us part good friends—one last kiss even, if you like. I took you to amuse me. You have not perhaps succeeded very well, but, after all, you have done what you could. You have been pleasant enough in your Japanese way." She prostrates herself, her forehead on the threshold of the door, till he is out of sight. He turns once or twice to look at her, but it is a mere civility merited by her grand final salutation.

Later . . . "In my cabin, one evening, in the midst of the Yellow Sea, my eyes chance to fall upon the lotus brought from Diu-jen-ji. They had lasted for two or three days, but now they are faded and pitifully strew my carpet with their pale pink petals.

"I have carefully preserved a good many faded flowers, fallen into dust, stolen here and there at moments of parting in different parts of the world. I have treasured so many that the collection is almost a herbarium. Now I will try hard to get up a sentiment for these—and they are the last living souvenirs of my summer at Nagasaki.

"I pick them up, not unkindly, however, and open my porthole. From the grey misty sky, a livid light falls upon the waters, a wan and gloomy kind of twilight creeps down yellowish upon this Yellow Sea, and I throw the poor lotus into the boundless waste of waters, apologizing for bestowing them, natives of Japan, in a grave so solemn and so vast."

The note of irony on which he concludes is rare, and marks the depth of his contempt.

From Che-fu on the Chinese coast, Yves was sent home, sick, to France. His departure created a void around Loti. He strove to fill it, as we know, by directing his thoughts to his homeland, by concentrating his attention upon his second novel of Breton life. He had contemplated that work as far back as the March of that year, as a letter inquiring about the methods of the Iceland fisheries sufficiently attests; but just as the hues of Constantinople appeared brighter under the winter skies of Morbihan, so Brittany and its people became dearer when remembered in the eastern seas. In the Yellow

Sea, of his new-found tenderness for France, was born Gaud, finest of French heroines.

But he had by no means seen the last of Japan. After a month's stay at Che-fu, his ship returned to Japanese waters, and for two months was cruising along those coasts. Loti made no effort to renew his marriage with Okane-San. He found other things to interest him than the pursuit of women. He visited Kyoto, the holy city, and Nikko, the sacred mountain. At thirty-five years of age, his eyes had opened wider to the manifold interests of this world. And beneath the thick veneer of Japanese reserve and artificiality, his compassionate eye detected a real human nature and simple rustic tenderness. In the *Chanson des Epoux* he tells the story of a poor Japanese couple, whose love survived poverty, age, and death. The husband is blind; his wife is paralysed; and he drags her about the streets of Nagasaki on a handcart. One day, the woman dies. She is buried on the spot. The blind man puts himself once more between the shafts and trots on, drawing the empty vehicle. He can only do what he has been accustomed to do and goes on . . . into a yet darker night.

Japan had found a way to Loti's heart through the ever-open door of his compassion.

Still, he left it, I imagine, with no regrets, on November 17th, 1885, when the *Triomphante* was headed for France. He reached Toulon on February 10th following.

CHAPTER XIII

MARRIAGE. LOTI AND A QUEEN

EVEN the sailor must find at last that the wives in every port end by resembling each other strangely. Memories become for him more satisfying than new experiences. In his thirty-seventh year, Loti found the author gaining on the amorist. His work shows this *Pêcheur d'Islande* is written with greater care, with more regard for the canons of the art, than any of his earlier works. And this time, for the length of a whole novel, he was able, almost entirely, to forget himself.

Indeed, he had taken so much trouble with his last book that though the first chapters were published in the *Nouvelle Revue* on March 15th, 1886, it was not till after Mme. Adam's first visit to his home at Rochefort, at Easter, that he sent her the concluding instalments. His industry was rewarded. *Pêcheur d'Islande* established him as one of the first masters of French fiction. Even Maxime Gaucher, hitherto among the least friendly of his critics, hailed the novel as a masterpiece, adding, "It is a simple story, a commonplace story; but told by Pierre Loti it is a *chef-d'œuvre*. That is precisely the secret of Pierre Loti. He imparts to everything, men and things, such an intensity of life, such relief, so much movement and so much colour, that we do not read of them, we see them. Before we have turned over more than a few pages, his characters have become old friends. His style has a transparency, so much suppleness and elasticity, that the thought itself is at once vividly apparent. This marvellous style conveys not only the idea of the thing, but the sensation."

The book has long ago passed into the literature of the world. His stories of the sea commended Loti, to people whom, in that age, his erotic confessions would have shocked profoundly. *Yves* was translated into English by Major Fletcher, and published by Vizetelly in 1887; Maxwell's introduced *The Iceland Fisherman* to the English public the next year. (The English title is misleading. It suggests that the hero belonged to the race beloved of Hall Caine, *Fishers of the North* would be better).

I do not know whether others have said the same, but to me it seems strange that this, the really great epic of the sea, should have been written by a Frenchman. Joseph Conrad, in the opinion of some, might dispute the palm, but he, again, was not an Englishman. The struggle of our British fishermen, with a sea as unfriendly as Iceland's, has not yet found a Loti.

"The success of *Rarahu*," says the author's French biographer, "directed public attention to *Aziyade*, which obtained the same warm reception. It seemed unlikely that an author could maintain himself at the same level of success. Yet Loti did so. One after the other, he produced other novels, other romances, and other narratives of travel, which met with equal favour." This may be true; but they were not of equal merit. Loti has ceased to live romances, and writes no more real novels. His power of observation becomes more acute, his circle of interests widens; but he draws ever more and more on his stock of memories, till they weary us by repetition.

It was at this stage of his career that Loti appropriately enough determined to marry. His bride, who was not chosen for him by Juliette Adam, was Mademoiselle Jeanne Blanche Franc de Ferrière, a member of an old Bordeaux family. No details of the courtship have been communicated to the public, and the marriage itself, which was celebrated on October 20th, 1886, seems to have come as a surprise to the world of letters. Nobody could imagine Loti a husband, a family man. His motive, M. Serban thinks, is clear enough. Tortured by his horror of annihilation, he sought to perpetuate himself otherwise than by his books. He wished to have children. That purpose was fulfilled in February, 1889, by the birth of his son, Samuel, who became the devoted friend and loyal collaborator of his father.

Of Mme. Viaud we hear very little. The honeymoon was spent in Spain. Loti, writing to Mme. Adam from Granada, on November 2nd, 1886, speaks of "his charming little wife." I have not traced many more references to her in his letters and diaries so far published, nor did his visit to Andalusia on this occasion inspire so much as a magazine article. Without impertinence, we are justified in concluding that his marriage did not rank in Loti's mind as one of his idylls.

"The devotion of Mme. Viaud," says Serban, "her abnegation as steadfast as it was discreet, her deliberate self-effacement, in a word, that heroism so necessary to the wife of a great author, which she possessed in a high degree, enabled Loti to resume more or less his old way of life."

He did not, for instance, leave the navy, though he was content the first three or four years of his married life with port duties, which kept him at or near Rochefort. Still less did it occur to him to transplant himself and his nascent family to Paris. He bought a house at Hendaye, which looked across at Spain; but spent most of his time at the house where he was born, where his mother and Aunt Claire still lived. His attachment to the scenes of his childhood never waned. I suspect that he had ever before his eyes the picture sketched out that April evening as he sat in his "museum" dreaming of his future. Since the old home was too sacred to abandon or to rebuild, he enlarged it by the simple expedient of buying and adding to it the houses right and left. The combined interior, with the wealth acquired by his pen, and possibly in part by marriage, he embellished and transformed, creating a vast mediæval hall, and an imitation mosque. But he religiously preserved the "museum." The stage must remain set for the last act.

On July 5th, 1887, Loti was enrolled in the Legion of Honour. He had earned the distinction more by his services to literature than as an officer; but he had quite recovered the good opinion of his chiefs. His old captain of the *Triomphante* placed it on record that Lieutenant Viaud was not one of those officers who neglected their duty in order to cultivate talents unconnected with their profession. He was devoted to the service, animated by zeal and activity. Admiral Prizbuier agreed, observing that M. Viaud's high literary reputation should not be allowed to obscure his merits as a naval officer.

Loti affected to receive this "bit of ribbon" with utter indifference. "In my present distress of mind," he informed Juliette Adam, "I would have preferred a black cloth to shroud myself in." Much sweeter, no doubt, were the marks of favour he was now to receive from a foreign sovereign.

This was Paulina Elizabeth, queen of Carol I. of Rumania. Like her husband, she was German by birth and education, but a German princess animated, one might say, by the traditions of Weimar. In the 'eighties and 'nineties of the last century she came in for a large share of public curiosity and sympathy. She had endeared herself to her husband's semi-barbarous subjects by nursing the wounded in the war of '78, and had since busied herself with developing their culture. Her good sense is shown by a passage in one of her later letters. (December 13th, 1901) : "There is something terribly false in our position [that of sovereigns]. And yet it seems as if people on a certain level of culture

CARMEN SYLVA.

wanted some demigod to look up to!* But the
mission is often dreary and very fatiguing. To be
a little Buddha always is not at all gay!"

Not satisfied with a crown, therefore, the queen
coveted literary distinction. Under the pseudonym,
which was certainly no disguise, of Carmen Sylva,
she published various books, one of which appeared
in Paris entitled *Thoughts of a Queen* (*Les Pensées
d' une Reine*). The thoughts were not very profound, nor were her books generally interesting.
But Queen Elizabeth was a very fine woman, and
her devotion to letters was sincere.

She knew no national prejudice in this matter,
and entertained a warm admiration for the great
French writers of the day, though she held that the
English alone knew how to write novels. In Loti
she saw an exception to this rule. She liked his
work so much that through her favourite, Helen
Vacaresco, she sent him a copy of her poem *Jehovah*
translated into French. Loti did not care for
poetry, but, possibly because he knew the author
to be a queen, or at any rate a woman, he sent back
a flattering acknowledgment. Being then informed
definitely that Carmen Sylva was the Queen of
Rumania, he begged her to accept a copy of *Pêcheur
d'Islande*, which had just been published (dedicated
it should be observed, to Juliette Adam).

The queen liked the book so much that she set
to work to translate it into German. At the same
time, she asked the author to visit her at Sinaia,

* It is not to be supposed that the queen had any other country than Roumania
in mind.

in the Carpathian mountains. I do not imagine that Loti had any hesitation about accepting the invitation. He was drawn not only by the powerful spell of royalty, but also by the opportunity of revisiting the scene of his loves with Aziyade. This double pilgrimage was undertaken, be it remarked, within less than a year of his marriage. No difficulty seems to have been placed in his way by the naval authorities.

Loti has left us an account of his reception in his sketch, *L'Exilée*. It was not published, however, till 1893, and must be checked by comparison with the version given by another eye-witness. This was Helen Vacaresco, afterwards a well-known literary character, and a somewhat romantic figure, of whom our author must be pardoned for speaking a trifle patronizingly. Her first impressions of Loti she communicated casually and without malice to a Hungarian journalist, who promptly turned them into copy. Other details she supplied to M. Serban, who, himself a professor at a Rumanian university, must be accepted as our most reliable authority on Loti's relations with the Rumanian queen.

Wearing a grey suit and a flower in his buttonhole, Loti was met at Bukarest, on September 27th, by Her Majesty's secretary. He was shown the tomb of the queen's daughter, who had died in her childhood ten years before, and then proceeded to Sinaia. In the course of his wanderings, the author had seen even more beautiful and picturesque spots, but at this moment the royal residence, Castel Peles, towered before his delighted eyes like an enchanted castle of some Arthurian legend. The honoured guest of a queen, housed beneath the same roof with her, he, no doubt, glanced backward over his whole life and told himself that the glamorous vision of his boyhood was even being transcended.

Only a very fine line divides the grand manner from the theatrical. When Louis Philippe saw the coffin of Napoleon approaching, instead of waiting for it, he jumped up and ran to meet it. That, of course, was a fine gesture—one hopes it was unpremeditated. Loti was received in after years in a very different fashion by an English sovereign. But the Queen of Rumania liked to do fine things in a fine way. She realized that she and Loti were eminently picturesque personages, and stage-managed their meeting accordingly.

"In a vast Gothic hall, furnished with high carved stalls, the ladies-in-waiting were grouped round their queen. Draped in white, a costume which admirably suited her wonderful white hair and rosy cheeks, Carmen Sylva was seated at the organ, playing a melancholy prelude of Bach.

"Upon the entrance of Loti, she rose and advanced to meet him, holding the manuscript of her translation of his work. Her manner was that of a queen; but her ineffable smile, her affectionate voice, spoke cordiality. The Queen of Rumania was doing honour to an illustrious confrère."

Loti, we are not surprised to hear, found himself unprepared for this reception. A minute or two elapsed before he was entirely at his ease.

Meanwhile, so Helen Vacaresco afterwards told the Hungarian journalist, his appearance had produced a feeling of disappointment in the maids of honour, if not in the queen herself. Loti's photograph had not apparently reached Bukarest. They had pictured the lover of Rarahu and Aziyade, the hardy, irresistible sailor, the devil-may-care comrade of "Frère Yves," as—well, as a romantic young lady would picture him. Instead, they saw a small gentleman built up on high heels, with a plaintive, somewhat undistinguished countenance, which he had, most unfortunately, endeavoured to embellish by means of cosmetics. (This was in days long before the Rumanian war office forbade officers *under the rank of major* to paint their faces). Nor was this unassuming presence corrected by a debonair manner. But as his shyness wore off, and he began to talk, the queen and her ladies perceived the charm of the man, and fell under the spell of his discourse. Probably they all felt the truth of the quatrain which not one of them had ever heard: "The mind's the standard of the man."

Unconscious of that momentary bad impression, the author unbosomed himself to Carmen Sylva, and revelled in the intimate atmosphere of royalty. Each professed to find the other a kindred soul. "They proposed to write in collaboration superhuman masterpieces. The Queen," adds M. Serban cruelly, "with a facility which often impaired her style, immediately dashed off numerous pages. Loti stopped short at the intention."

He was presented to King Carol, who was not a

man of his stamp, but for whom he has a good word. He rambled through the forests with the Queen, talked, and played music with her, and witnessed the national dances. Carmen Sylva at times wore the native costume. Loti departed from Sinaia, dazzled by her personality, by his environment, and perhaps a little by her crown. Spenser's tributes to Gloriana are cold and niggardly in comparison with his to the queen of Rumania.

They met again at Bukarest in 1890 and in the summer of the following year at Venice. It was before setting out for the latter place that Loti heard of that unpleasant description of himself in a Hungarian paper. It was obvious that the details had been supplied by someone at the court. He wrote to the queen's secretary, complaining that nothing in his whole life had occasioned him so much pain and vexation. "The thing," he added, "will make the round of the Press, and go down to posterity. If I really look like that, up till now I have always found myself in the company of people too kind-hearted and too well-bred to tell me so. It has been reserved for this young person to let me know it."

Whether he meant Helen Vacaresco by the young person, is not clear. At all events, when he found her, as usual, in attendance upon the queen at the Hotel Danieli, at Venice, there was no appearance of a quarrel between them. But he speaks of her with no excess of cordiality. Seated at the queen's feet, in a simple pink dress, was Mademoiselle Helen Vacaresco, "her black eyes, keen and inquisitive. She posed as the spoiled child of that adorable mother. Already I had noticed that, in the absence of an audience, her manner towards the queen became colder and more distant. This is not said to her discredit—so few women are able to appear perfectly natural. Her attachment to her mother by adoption was no doubt sincere, and the grief she was to feel at parting from her for ever was undoubtedly bitter."

It was on account of this sprightly young lady that Carmen Sylva found herself practically in banishment at Venice. The queen had smiled upon the love which had grown up between her son—the actual king of Rumania—and her gifted protégé. More: she sanctioned an engagement between them, and wanted the marriage to take place. Great was the wrath of her husband, King Carol. Strange to say, his indignation was shared by his subjects, who held that a prince of the line of Hohenzollern should not disgrace himself by marrying one of themselves. This singular attitude is not confined to the Rumanians—it was expressed, to some extent, in our own Royal Marriage Act, and more recently when the Serbs murdered their king very largely because he had married a Serbian woman.

From Venice, Queen Elizabeth was still urging her son to play, what she considered, the only honourable part, or at least to return to Helen her ring and love-letters. The eyes of all Europe (which just then had nothing much else to think about) were turned upon the little circle in the Hotel Danieli. With unfeigned amusement, Helen read out the repeated announcements of her own suicide. "Not that I would condescend to that," she commented sharply. "It would be the act of a jilted housemaid." As to Loti, he could not be expected to wish for the aggrandisement of Mlle. Vacaresco. He was not romantic in the English sense, and evidently believed, like most of his countrymen, that marriages should be arranged by the family on a business-like basis. All his sympathy was for the queen, who found herself at loggerheads with her husband and her people. During that August in Venice he took every opportunity of assuring her of his regard, his loyalty, and his admiration. He enjoyed the long gondola excursions, the serenades by moonlight, the delightfully appropriate setting of Venice. The faithful troubadours must have come into his mind. Perhaps he had heard of Chatelard or of Rizzio. And indeed the friendship, though it did not end tragically, ended sadly.

When Carmen Sylva had given way, and Helen Vacaresco had been banished for ever from Rumania, Loti chivalrously published a panegyric and defence of his royal friend, under the title of *Une exilée*. Thereupon, King Carol, "who," says M. Serban, "never knew how to pardon anyone," absolutely forbade his wife to hold any communication whatsoever with the Frenchman. But Carmen Sylva never forgot Loti. There seems to have been "a furtive exchange of books and autographed portraits, by means of occasional intermediaries"— quite after the manner of Ruritania ' "Aging, both of them, they exchanged the memory of an unalterable friendship across the intervening space."

I see no reason to question the reality of this attachment. Presumably a queen may be liked for her own sake. As a final proof of his sincerity, it is not necessary to advance Loti's refusal to abuse his old friend because, in 1914, she took the part of her own countrymen. "In the shock of war, when Rumanians and Frenchmen contemned the queen, what nobleness of soul does not this defence indicate on his part!" exclaims Serban. This seems to me nonsense. Loti would have been a miserable worm, indeed, if he despised a woman for sticking to her own compatriots. As it is, ridiculously enough, he feels called upon to offer excuses for her having done so. The war spirit was often as poor stuff as the petrol supplied under that name.

We share M. Serban's regret that, in his pre-occupation with the queen, Loti paid so little attention to the country. "Loti says nothing of the Rumanians, because he had no opportunity of knowing them; as to the country, he had no time to see it. He was aware, nevertheless, that there was a picturesque side to Rumania, which he ignored. In a letter addressed to Mlle. Helen Vacaresco, he announces his intention of one day hiding himself in some Rumanian village in order to study the simple life of the shepherds and peasants. He never executed that project."

CHAPTER XIV

THE SPECTRE OF HIS YOUTH

His first visit to the Queen of Rumania ended, Loti travelled, via Bukarest and Constanta, to Constantinople (October, 1887). He was drawn thither mainly by the hankering after the scenes of his youth, so strong in a man of his temperament. The narrative of this second visit to the Ottoman capital is contained in *Fantôme d'Orient*. It says much for Loti's popularity in the 'nineties that Calmann-Levy should have put such a book on sale. Not that its style or matter makes it unworthy of the author; but it is merely a short chapter of auto-biography, pages torn, one might suppose, from a man's diary, hardly worth anyone else's while to purchase. It might be entitled *What became of Aziyade*.

What had become of her? Loti, for what reason is not clear, seems to have made up his mind that she was dead. In his last letter, written from Lorient, he had advised her to marry a Turk if her old protector, Abeddin, should die. With the scents and sights of Constantinople, the past came back.

Memories of the Circassian girl he had loved ten years before surged up and washed out—for the moment—the other memories in which the intervening years had been so fruitful.

By choice or necessity, he had allowed himself only two days for this pilgrimage. Loti was an artist in these matters. He may have reflected that a longer stay might be productive of fresh associations and fresh memories, whereas he wanted to keep Stamboul and Aziyade exclusively and indissolubly associated in his mind.

All these years he had carefully treasured a slip of paper on which Achmet, a friend of those earlier days, had written, in Turkish character, the name and address of an Armenian woman, of whom at any future time inquiry after him or Aziyade might be made. The address was "Anaktar-Shiraz, at Kassim-Pasha, in a low house on the Hajji Ali square, next door to a fruit-seller's, opposite an old man who sells tarbushes."

This address Loti gave the morning after his arrival to a Greek guide, who found it precise enough. Then an anxious, heart-breaking search began. Loti conveys, even to those who have never had the like experience, the agonies of hope aroused and deferred, defeated and revived, his struggles with ignorance, laziness, and stupidity, the physical fatigue, one might almost say the dryness of his throat, as he pursued his quest through that gigantic human ant-hill.

Yes, the Greek knew the square of Hajji Ali at Kassim-Pasha very well. They got there. They found the house next door to the fruit-seller's. But Anaktar Shiraz had moved. She was now living out near the Jewish cemeteries at Pri-Pasha.

It took some time to get to this other suburb. They found the house, but could make no one hear. An old Jew, looking out of the next door window, inquired what they sought. "Anaktar Shiraz? Why, she had gone that day on a visit to a friend who lived next door to her old home at Kassim-Pasha!"

It was getting late, and in Turkey no sort of business or inquiries can be prosecuted after sundown. For the moment Loti forsook the search. He took a caïk (a Constantinople gondola) and went up the Golden Horn, to Eyub, to look at the house where he and Aziyade had loved each other so intensely. He should have remembered that it had been burnt down. With a deepened sense of the unfriendliness of time and things, Loti turned and looked long and earnestly at a near-by mosque. That at least, had been spared from those days.

Well, at last they found the Armenian, and when, with great trouble, the foreigner had recalled the dead Achmet to her recollection, she took him to see an old sister of Achmet's. The elderly lady insisted, first, on offering him coffee according to the sacred law of hospitality. She would know Hadije— Aziyade. Loti, nerving himself, mentioned the beloved name, then asked, to spare himself a shock, "She is dead, is she not?"

The Turkish lady's manner implied, "Yes."

Well, he had known it, or guessed it all along. He asked where she was buried.

But that Achmet's sister could not tell him. With enormous pains they tracked down an old negress who had been employed in the household of Abeddin Effendi. They found her, ragged, diseased, aged, in a wretched hovel. At the mention of her former mistress's name, she looked reproachfully at the giaour. She holds me guilty of her death, he thought. Bestirring her aching bones, the poor old crone conducted him to a corner of the great cemetery near the Seven Towers. There were several women's tombs. "Burda, burda!" ("Here, here!") cried the negress, pointing. And Loti leaning forward read the name of his dead love in gilt letters on a blue tomb.

How had she died? "I could not believe," says Loti, "that a young woman, apparently vigorous, could die of grief alone." She had been dead, the negress told him with a supreme effort at recollection, seven years. Abeddin Effendi had discovered Aziyade's intrigue with the Frank. He had not maltreated her, but had confined her in disgrace to her rooms. The negress remembered to have given her the first six letters she had received from Loti. The others?—those she had burnt, when she was dismissed by Abeddin upon her complicity being detected. As to letters addressed by Aziyade to Loti, she had posted only four. Loti reflected. He had received others in a style which, he noticed at the time, was odd and different. Who then had written them? . . . He was never to know.

"But how came she to die?"

The negress did not know. She was not there. But it was cold that spring of 1880, and Aziyade's room was very cold. There was no need to inquire further.

Next day, Loti paid his sacramental visit alone to her tomb. Then he went away from Constantinople. So she was dead. She had died in her cold room, grieving for him. "And in what part of the world was I," he asks frantically, "that I did not hear her call, that I did not hurry to save her?"

That question is easily answered. More difficult to say is exactly what he had hoped to find in thus re-visiting the scenes of that dead passion. Supposing, for instance, that Aziyade had still been alive?

CHAPTER XV

LOTI returned to Rochefort, dedicated a species of shrine to his dead Turkish love in his oriental chamber, and, while eternally mourning the irrecoverable past, seems to have extracted a reasonable amount of enjoyment out of the present. His visit to the castle in the midst of the Carpathians gave him a taste for what may be called feudal romance, which hitherto had not been remarked in him. In the splendid Gothic hall of his house he organized, in April, 1888, a mediæval fête, which is recorded in the newspapers of the time as an event of almost national importance. Loti, assisted by the students of the Ecole des Chartes, had devoted six months to the preparation of it. The hosts and the guests all wore the costume of the year 1470. "Pierre Loti, dressed as Louis XI, seated on a dāis, had on his right the lovely Beatrice of Gif"—so runs the account in the *Illustration*. This lady was no other than Juliette Adam, who had just bought the ancient abbey of Gif. "Madame Loti, on another dāis, faced him, between *Tiel*, the Duke of Bur-

LOTI'S HOUSE AT ROCHEFORT:
FIRE-PLACE IN THE GREAT HALL.

LOTI'S HOUSE AT ROCHEFORT:
THE ARABIAN ROOM.

gundy's fool, and *Maistre Coictier*, the King's physician." The banquet that followed was in true mediæval style, consisting of thirteen courses. The dishes were so strange to the nineteenth century palate that aids to digestion were judiciously interposed. At the proper moment the picturesque crowd drank the health of Pierre Loti and his noble lady in goblets of champagne. "Beatrice de Gif," pronounced a discourse in French of Louis XI's time, hardly understanding a word of it herself. The inhabitants of Rochefort were admitted to witness the splendid scene and pay homage to their illustrious townsman, seated on his dāis! The festivities concluded with a ball by torchlight. Loti understood the king business better than Carmen Sylva.

Meantime he had written *Propos d'Exil*, published in 1887—a work which Sir Edmund Gosse considers has not been appreciated at its true value—several important magazine articles, and *Madame Chrysanthème*, which first appeared in December, 1887. His naval duties, fortunately, were by no means arduous. In September, 1888, he obtained what seems to have been his first command—of a little boat, the *Ecureuil*, stationed permanently at Rochefort! In the following March the *wanderlust* moved him. He got leave for two months, and immediately after the birth of his son, started off for Morocco, in company with M. Patenotre, who had been appointed French minister to his Sherifian Majesty.

Now and henceforward, he becomes a traveller— he goes out in search of new sights and impressions not in search of strange women and new loves. He hopes, of course, that these will happen; but the rôle of the mere observer is no longer definitely irksome to him. After all, middle life had brought with it substantial consolations. If one could not continue a young midshipman, making love to half-clad Maoris and veiled Circassians, it was no bad thing to be the eminent writer, Pierre Loti, travelling with an official mission, talking almost on a footing of equality with the great ones of the earth.

In those days, El Hasan, the Sultan or Sherif of Morocco, ranked as one of these. Loti eyed him with interest. "The last faithful representative of a religion, of a civilization (*sic*) in process of extinction. He is the personification of Old Islam—for the orthodox Muslims look on the Sultan of Stambul as little better than a sacrilegious usurper, and turn their eyes and their prayers towards Al Moghreb, towards the True Successor of the Prophet. . . . His brown, parchment-like face, framed in white draperies, has regular and noble features, and lacklustre eyes, the white of which shows below the half-hidden pupil. His expression is one of extreme melancholy, of supreme lassitude. . . . He seems mild, and is so, according to those who know him.* (In the opinion of the people of Fez, he is even too mild. He does not offer enough bloody sacrifices to the holy cause of Islam). But his is only a relative mildness, such as existed among us in the Middle Ages, which is not too much shocked by the shedding of blood or at the sight of a row of human heads

* This seems also to have been the European opinion of El Hasan IV.

above the gates of a palace. Still, he is not cruel. His sweet, sad air shows that. He chastises at times severely as his divine power entitles him to do, but he would rather pardon, so they say. . . . He is someone whom we, of this age, can neither understand nor judge; but he is very certainly someone great, someone imposing. . . ."

Any kind of royalty captivated Loti. He liked to endow this feeble princeling with the sublimest of virtues—charity; but elsewhere in this dreadful country he must have been very much at pains to reconcile what he saw with his favourable conception of Islam. He mentions without specific condemnation (which would indeed have been superfluous), but with a perceptible shrinking, the hideous indifference of these Muslims to animal life and human suffering. He could hardly have enjoyed his sojourn among these monsters. Their country reeked of blood. His book on Morocco should be carefully read by those who think the independence of these savage states should always be respected.

Returning to Rochefort, Loti resumed his duties on the *Ecureuil*. At the suggestion of Mme. Adam, or moved by his own ambition, he now aimed at the highest honour open to the French man of letters—membership of the Academy. He offered himself for election on May 1st, 1890, and received only five votes. He was encouraged to try again. Upon the death of his friend, Octave Feuillet, he was proposed for the vacant seat by Comte d'Haussonville, this time in opposition to the formidable Emile Zola. When it became evident that his candidature was to be taken seriously, the most violent antagonism manifested itself in quarters expected and un-expected. Literary jealousies are much more openly and ferociously pursued in France than amongst us, and are fomented, of course, by these recurring contests for the palm of the Academy. Lieutenant Viaud's success had exasperated many; his person-ality was repugnant to numbers of his own sex because of his popularity with the other; he was derided as the candidate of the women, of the salons, even of the clericals. In addition, not a few honestly favoured Zola, and considered the sailor-romancer unworthy of the vacant fauteuil.

"Camille Doucet and Dumas are my worst enemies in the assembly," wrote Loti to Juliette Adam. To disarm the opposition of the former he asks her to proclaim "the correctness of his private life." "My way of living," he asserts, "has never shocked any but fools who did not look close enough." "The 'doux Camille' has set himself to spread stupid yarns, which, of course, I cannot bring home to him, and which, indeed, I disdain to follow up." On April 21st he despairs of conciliating "le doux Camille", but relies much on the support of the Duc d'Aumale. Meanwhile, a passionate campaign was carried on in the press for and against his nomination.

He was elected on May 21st, 1891, by thirty-six votes against three cast for the apostle of naturalism. He was informed of the result at Algiers. Having relinquished his derisory command, he was now serving on the *Formidable*, cruising about the western Mediterranean. One of his letters is headed

Ajaccio; it was at Toulon that Carmen Sylva's last invitation reached him.

The ceremony of his reception into the Academy took place in the following year on April 7th. The séance was very well attended, among others by Mme. Carnot, the president's wife, by Lord Dufferin, the British ambassador, by Daudet, Sarcey, Claretie, Lavedan, Zola, the defeated candidate and a host of literary and social celebrities. His election was treated by the *Figaro* as a victory for the salons. Introduced by Ernest Renan and Sully Prudhomme, Loti, according to custom, pronounced the panegyric of his predecessor, Feuillet. In the course of his speech, which was badly delivered, he startled the assembly by the admission, "I never read. This is true—as a result of intellectual indolence, of some unaccountable fear of the written thought, or of some mental lassitude, I do not read." He did not refrain from some criticism of the school opposed to him, and spoke scathingly of naturalism. Zola, in the gallery was observed to smile.

That night, Juliette Adam organised an apotheosis of her protégé, which was attended by the "Tout-Paris." Flushed with victory, the new Academician could afford to smile at a bitter article directed against him in the *Figaro*, signed by Maurice Barrés. He was taunted with his narrowness of ideas, his want of culture, and sensuality—told, also, that he had been accepted by the assembly only because Bourget and de Maupassant had declined to stand. To all this, an admirer of Loti may be forgiven for retorting that this author of limited culture, at his worst, has never

written anything so bad as certain short stories by
M. Barrés.

But Pierre Loti, member of the Academy, remained
only Lieutenant Viaud. He could not very well
qualify for promotion in the salons of Paris or in the
study, but still he clung to the navy, seldom appearing out of uniform. At last a job was found for him.
He was appointed to command the *Javelot*, a little
gunboat stationed, on what was practically coastguard duty at the mouth of the Bidassoa, close to
his new home at Hendaye.

According to his letters, he would have preferred
to take to the high seas again, but did not dare to
leave his mother in her declining years. In December, 1890, she had lost her life's companion, her
sister Claire. Loti had loved his aged aunt, next, I
fancy, to his mother. In her he lost another link
with the youth to which he clung so passionately;
in her death, he had another reminder of the common
fate to which he could not reconcile himself. It was
the first time he had witnessed the calm, ordered
passing of an aged person under the domestic roof;
for the first time he saw a coffin brought into the
house where he was born. In his minute, vivid
account of *Tante Claire's* last moments, he still
abstains from any reference to the death of his father
which had taken place during one of his first cruises.

"On day I shall be like that," was Loti's immediate
thought, on being brought face to face with the dead.
Apparently, among his beloved Muslims, he had
never heard the saying attributed to them by
Matthew Arnold, "There is nothing the wise man

thinks of less than death." He thought of it always, and he thought of it with horror. Swinburne's beautiful lines would have been incomprehensible to him. Death for him was not a sleep, but a nightmare. I wonder what he would have said of an odd forgotten poem (by Philip Bourke-Marston, if I remember rightly), which expresses the despair of men on learning that "death is dead." "To think that even yesterday we might have died!" is the reflection that tortures them most. It is not much of an exaggeration to say, on the contrary, that this French author hardly thought life worth living, since it had to end. He would not, as the sage advises, rise up from life as from a banquet, with thanks to the giver—he reproached the giver for not letting him sit on. By the way, if I am not mistaken, he makes no reference to suicide in all his works—yet he should have been reminded of it by the suicide of General Boulanger, the most prominent political figure of his time. Loti had, it might be argued, every reason to be in love with life; but he would have been the last to admit that, and nothing can be surer than that he would have clung to life equally if he had been a slave under the horrible Romans.

"What I like best in your dream," he wrote to his "second mother," "is this faith in the persistence after death of friendship and love, of the union of two souls. What is most odious, what revolts me most in the conception of final annihilation is precisely that it extinguishes those unions which are the only sublime things given by life." Yet he had seen a good many of those unions extinguished in life. The death of the beloved old woman caused him to reach out more eagerly than before for the gift of faith. Islam could not give him what he sought—it accorded only dubiously a post-mortem existence to Aziyade, in Marocco it saturated itself, like the old Jewish religion, in the slowly-distilled blood of tortured and innocent beasts. Loti turned once more to Christianity—not in the form he had known it in childhood, not to the religion of the Trappists—he would seek it at its cradle in the beloved East.

The expedition was, in fact, meditated and planned a long time ahead. "Elaborate negotiations with the Arab sheiks assured Loti of a cordial reception, and a substantial escort for the dangerous regions he must traverse. He was accompanied by Leo Théméze, a comrade, and by the Duc de Dino, who went no farther than Jerusalem." The name of Leo Théméze occurs several times in the correspondence with Mme. Adam. He was a young sailor who had had a lot of hard luck, and was now trying to get a master's ticket in the merchant service. Loti, as usual, made his friend's interests his own, and he was again invoking Mme. Adam's boundless good nature to get round some technical obstacle which barred Leo's path. The obstacle was overcome. Loti's letters teach us that almost anything could be done by influence at the French Ministry of Marine in those days. How many promotions, I wonder, have not been settled at Maxim's, so conveniently opposite!

The pilgrims set out in February, 1894. To a reporter of a Rochefort paper, Loti confessed his misgivings. "To approach the very source of Christianity, the birthplace of all religions (*sic*), one needs the faith and the soul of one's childhood. To those I cannot pretend. Perhaps a disappointment is in store for me. I have been warned that Jerusalem has become appallingly commonplace, now that it boasts a railway and a lift to the summit of Calvary is even talked of."

A complete caravan, with camels, tents, Arab flute-players, and guards awaited the party near Cairo. The Frenchmen donned the burnous and headdress of Arabs, passing among Muslims for pilgrims from El Moghreb. They crossed the canal and made for the desert in which the Israelites had wandered. On the slopes of the terrific mountain of Sinai they pitched their camp in the snow. High above towered the ramparts of the monastery. Thanks to a letter of introduction from the Patriarch of Cairo, the party were admitted after nightfall within those precincts, "which the situation of the desert has preserved from revolutions, from pillage, from all renovations, in much the same state that they were left by the Emperor Justinian in the year 550." Bare-footed the travellers enter the chapel in the crypt, and are shown the rock where the angel of the Lord spoke to Moses from the Burning Bush. Turning his eyes away from the spot consecrated by tradition, Loti looks at the queer Byzantine effigies and muses on the flight of ages.

Moses casts no spell over the minds of men any more. If Loti really hoped to know God, it was not at Sinai. Nor yet at Hebron, where sleeps the common father of Arabs and Israelites, jealously screened from the impious gaze of all unbelievers. So at last the pilgrims came to Bethlehem in the hill country of Judea.

It is known, well enough, nowadays, the very birthplace of the Christ, to the myriads who offer Him so doubtful and dishonouring an allegiance. The tourists—*les Cooks*—whose presence vexed Loti and all other writers so much—most of our men of letters—thousands of soldiers—have familiarised London, Melbourne, Sydney, by word of mouth, with every detail of its configuration and condition. In 1906, I, at least, experienced no rude shock of disillusionment when a little native girl took me simply by the hand and showed me round the quiet mediæval-built town. But in 1894, the too-fastidious soul of Loti was outraged by the simple, practical arrangements made by "common Italian monks" for pilgrims less fortunately circumstanced than he. "Where are we now?" he asks. "In some suburban inn or restaurant? We had been warned, it is true, but we did not expect this. Oh, why did we come—why did we not return to the desert whence we beheld Bethlehem, still mysterious and beautiful?"

Assuredly, this was not the faith which could remove mountains. We have revealed here in Loti that ugly trait of snobbishness which prosperity increasingly strengthened. Perhaps he wanted a private view of Bethlehem! In the quiet of his

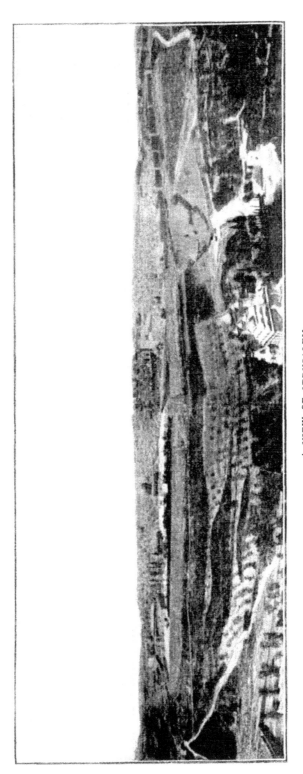

A VIEW OF JERUSALEM.

comfortable tent, a suspicion of this occurred to him. "Behind all this, there is always the Christ, unexplained and ineffable, who let the simple and the little ones approach him, who, if he was approaching these half-idolatrous worshippers, these Russian peasants, with tapers in their hands and tears in their eyes, would open his arms to welcome them."

At Jerusalem, in the church of the Holy Sepulchre, he saw again those Russian pilgrims. And watching them, he ceased to trouble about the nasty English tourists and the inartisticalness of it all. He breaks out, "May this spot be blessed, this strange unique spot called the Holy Sepulchre—doubtful, fictitious, if you like, but to which, these fifteen centuries past, the desolate multitudes have hastened, where hard hearts have melted like snow, where now my eyelids droop in an uprush of prayer, illogical if you wish, but ineffable and infinite . . ."

Of Gethsemane, he thought the monks had made something mean and vulgar. But as a later traveller, G. K. Chesterton, has so well said, they have done with it what children would have done—turned it into a garden full of flowers. So it was not to the garden but to a spot close by that Loti went by night in a desperate, calculated attempt to believe. He stretched himself on the ground against the roots of an olive tree, waiting, as he tells us, he knew not for what.

"Yet, my speechless prayer was suppliant and profound, and I was come from out much tribulation, from the abysses of anguish . . .

"No, nothing. No one sees me, no one hears me, no one answers. . .

"I wait. The moments pass, and with them my last confused hopes, carrying me into nothingness. . . ."

The moment had indeed passed. Emotion, imagination, the spell of the Great One who had suffered there, vainly assailed the stronghold of reason. Loti looked at the sky and found it of brass.

He turned again toward Islam, finding in the Mosque of Omar a refuge which suited him, "a place of dreams, which does not wring the heart, but which calms and enchants." He watched the Jews praying outside the wall of the Temple— watched them with dislike and contempt, with that antipathy which is natural to most Frenchmen. He visited Jericho and the Dead Sea. Leaving the Holy City, he addresses these words to those who may come after him. "Seek Him, you also, try . . . for outside of Him is nothing. To meet Him you have no need to come to Jerusalem, because, if He exists, He is everywhere. Perhaps you will succeed better than I have done. At any rate, I bless that short moment when I so nearly recovered in Him hope ineffable and profound— however black the void seemed on the morrow."

He went north to Galilee, that pleasant country of flowery hillsides, and, strange to say, perceived something melancholy in his first view of red-roofed Nazareth. He looked down on the little town as Jesus must so often have done. "Was there any room in his heart for any human fondness for His native soil—in that heart so much wider than our love of country? The Nazareth of His time, which showed itself so blindly hostile because He was of it, which drove Him away—no, He could not care for Nazareth, but perhaps for these fields of grass and flax . . . Who knows? At Gethsemane, at Golgotha, in that awful hour when all that was human in Him recoiled in terror before approaching dissolution, perhaps He saw, as the least of us will do, the familiar mountains of His childhood, and the high pastures where He used to await the signal for the shepherds to return."

But never again was Julien Viaud to hear the signal for him to re-enter the fold in which he had been baptised.

CHAPTER XVI

INDIA (WITHOUT THE ENGLISH)

NOT resuming the command of his guardship till 1896, Loti devoted himself in the eighteen months following his return from Palestine to writing his impressions, which he embodied in the volumes entitled " Le Désert," " Jerusalem," and "Galilee." His meditations upon religion were diversified by excursions into the vigorous, highly-coloured life of his Basque neighbours. With something like relief, I imagine, he turned to the adventures of the lusty smugglers and their robust loves. His sympathies, as always, took a practical shape. We find him appealing to his long-suffering friend, Mme. Adam, to obtain from the authorities in Paris a mitigation of the penalties inflicted on one of his contrabandist friends—a queer friend for the officer commanding a coastguard vessel! *Ramuntcho*, first published as a serial in the *Revue de Paris*, at the end of 1896, was rather in the vein of *Frère Yves ;* but Loti could not do for the peasantry of the western Pyrenees what he had done for the seafaring folk of Britanny.

His more cheerful mood was dispelled in May, 1897, by the worst blow which had ever been dealt him. His mother died, at the age of eighty-seven. To Juliette Adam, he writes simply, "I have lost my mother." He, so fluent, in his grief was left bankrupt of words by the loss of the being he had always loved before all others. He may have found an outlet for his sorrow in private letters; but if so, these outpourings have been properly held sacred by his correspondents, unless we except the letter to Mme. Adam, dated from Japanese waters, January 31st, 1901, in which he says, "The time, alas, has gone by when I feared that if a cruise were too long I might find her gone upon my return—her, whose place no one can ever fill. But now it matters little how long I am away, since I shall not find her awaiting me when I do return."

To the day of his own death, her room was kept just as she might have left it in the morning, the bed made, her workbox open. In the house, transformed into a palace, where, from the Baronial Hall, you pass into chambers recalling the gorgeous East, the family sitting-room was left untouched in all its 1830 ugliness, as in the days when his father and mother sat with their first child before the hearth.

It is significant that he wrote nothing during the rest of that year, but the article "Inutile Pitié" afterwards included in the volume *Réflets sur la Sombre Route*. Grief and years quickened his pity. In this last book we find included that article, "Mes dernières chasses," which I hope will remain and be read, together with *The Book of Pity and Death*, even if all his other work is forgotten.

Compassion, to speak a platitude, is the emotion excited in one by the suffering of another creature. It is essentially indiscriminate, and leads inevitably to seeming inconsistencies. Loti professed for the greater part of his life to hate the English; yet it ought to have struck him, in the course of his wanderings about the world, that only among us is his sympathy with animals at all widely diffused and acted upon. Contrariwise, he appears to have liked the Spaniards, a people capable of signal magnanimity and generosity, it is true, but singularly insensible to the sufferings of the brute creation, perhaps as a result of their religious education. But Loti had no thought of the mangled horses of the bull-ring when war broke out between Spain and the United States. Like all other Frenchmen of that day, he was loudly and whole-heartedly on the side of the weaker power. He went to Madrid, and was received by the Queen-Regent. In the presence of this royalty of the first rank—by birth a Habsburg, by marriage a Bourbon, actually a ruling sovereign—he confesses himself overwhelmed. He would like to speak of her, but feels himself tongue-tied by awe. "Words fail me, I dare not write, because they could never be sufficiently respectful or discreet." It is a pity that the great French author was never given the opportunity of describing a royal christening or wedding in a London paper!

In fact, he liked kings almost as much as cats.

His fancy for them overleaped mere national prejudice. Someone offered to present him to

William II if he would go to Berlin. To the horror and indignation of Juliette Adam, who had passed all her life keeping alive the hatred of France for Germany, he went. He reasoned with her. These national prejudices were unreasonable—they were simply the result of environment—her antipathy for the Germanshad no better foundation than his for the English. . . . As things turned out, it was lucky for this determined courtier that, for reasons not clearly revealed to us, the promised presentation did not come off. But he did not speak ill of the Kaiser—who was, he believed, the enemy of those eternal enemies of France, the English. (In '99, Loti was shouting *Vive les Boêrs !* as loudly as the rest). He found it difficult to dislike the German people. He regards the Berliners drinking beer: "They were not antipathetic; nay, they had good-natured faces and carried courtesy farther than we do—the men remained bare-headed after having saluted every one in turn, salutes which were punctiliously returned. Our enemies, these people!" exclaims Loti, "but why or wherefore? How much of this national hatred is deliberately engineered, and how absurd are frontiers when these things are dispassionately considered!"

It is interesting, this conflict in Loti between his essential kindness and the patriotism which he recognises as artificial. For that patriotism is brusquely aroused by the sight of a French gun, now a German war trophy—a gun identical with those carried on a corvette he had served on. "I deceived myself just now. There are frontiers after all, and in spite of my serene detachment, I should remember that quickly enough at the first blast of war. For a long while yet, that old word 'patrie' will thrill us, and a flag of a particular colour will draw our souls after it. It may be antiquated —it may be ridiculous—but it is irresistible and perhaps sublime."

These words were written on shipboard in November, 1899. Loti was on his way to India. He was going, as he tells us, not out of a traveller's curiosity, but to seek enlightenment at the fountains of Aryan wisdom. In the last years of the nineteenth century, Europe was returning more and more towards the East for spiritual guidance. "Nirvana," "Karma," and "Yogi" were familiar words in London and Paris salons. Dimly recalling that movement, I have sometimes thought that Buddhism might have supplanted the European religion if it had not enjoined respect for animal life, that most inconvenient of virtues.

The account of what Loti saw and found in India is given in one of his larger books, published originally under the title of *L'Inde (sans les Anglais)*. In pursuance of his puerile animosity against a people whom he did not know, he had traced an ingenious itinerary across India, which avoided British territory as far as was possible and led for most of its length across the tributary states. From more than one point of view, he was wise. The Anglo-Indian has never extended a very cordial welcome to the literary traveller, and in the winter of '99 we were feeling very cross with foreigners. From the feudatory princes at Trivandrum, at Odaipur, at Jaipur, at Gwalior, everywhere, in fact, Loti was received with honour and lavish hospitality. That the fame of this purely French writer should have reached their highnesses puzzles me, as not impossibly it puzzled him. To the Maharaja of Travancore, the first potentate visited, he had an introduction, and, it may be conjectured, was furnished with letters from him to the other princes.

But he could not avoid the British dominions altogether, and had indeed to begin his journey in Ceylon. At Anaradhapura, Buddhism impressed him as a dead and perished thing, buried under ruins and the dust of ancient idols. On landing in India he was denied admission to the first Brahmin temple he encountered. A better impression was created by the strangely sequestered state of Travancore, "the Land of Charity," where men of all creeds lived in calm and freedom under the mildest of princes. But leaving the hospitable state on December 31st, 1899 (which, like so many other people, he persisted in thinking was the last day of the century), he complained that he had still seen nothing of the Hindu religion. At Tanjore, he saw the hideous idol of Ganesa and the procession of the car of Vishnu; at Madura, the great gilt palanquins of Siva and Parvati. After these orgies of idolatry he sought temporary relaxation at Pondicherry, that slumbering dependency of France, which lived still in the age of Louis XVI.

The flesh was very far from dead in him at fifty years of age, and he notices so many lovely shapes as he passes through India, that one half hopes he may meet with a Hindu Aziyade or some Eurasian Cora. The eyes of the dancing girls remind him of those which had first kindled passion in him, in that wood of Saintonge, long ago. But the bayadère at Pondicherry receives his compliments in a manner that is correct, cold, and indifferent, bowing and hiding her face with jewelled fingers. At Tanjore he approaches a beautiful girl of the highest caste, and helps her for a moment in decorating the route of a sacred procession, but withdraws quickly lest he be rebuffed. He wanders through the streets of the harlots at Benares, and admires their velvety eyes. But most he seems in love with a dead girl stretched on the funeral pyre. . . .

Death—he finds the abhorred spectre everywhere at his elbow, not only at its capital on the Ganges, but at every town and wayside station along his progress. For the famine is taking toll of millions. Little children thrust out reed-like arms, and struggle with each other almost in a death-agony for the coins the stranger throws them. "At each stopping-place a famished horde is waiting behind the barrier. The song we so dread to hear, that heart-rending, high-pitched, monotonous cry, greets us as we approach, swells, and rises into a desperate wail as we disappear into the parched desolate wastes."

The exquisite rose-coloured city of Jaipur is beseiged, encumbered, patrolled by starving wretches. "At this moment, they are piling sacks of rice on to the pavements . . . three starved and naked children, whose ages range from three to ten years, must be driven from the place where they had lain down to rest. A woman standing by tells us that their parents who brought them here are dead, of hunger, we suppose, and they stay because they have nowhere else to go. The woman appears to see nothing unusual in all this, she does not seem heartless or unkindly. My God, what sort of people are these? Of what material is their souls fashioned? They would not kill a bird, but feel no compunction when little children are left to die on their doorsteps."

Such a spectacle should have stifled any hopes the pilgrim might have had of Hinduism; but where death was so near at hand,* he thought he might look over its skinny shoulders into a beyond. At a temple near Udaipur, he talked, through an interpreter, of course, with two young Brahmins, priests, whose lineage dated back, without break or flaw, some two or three thousand years. Not for their pure descent or placid otherworldliness, but because they had never taken life in any form or eaten what had once lived, did they deserve respect. No, they could not give the reverent inquirer the assurances he sought. "I question them as to the nature of their hopes, and as to what they can see of the life beyond, but they cannot answer me in any way that I can understand. At once we lose touch with each other. A curtain like that of night falls between us. Doubtless they are seers, as indeed are the majority of priests (*sic*), but they are too simple-minded to explain themselves."

* He had taken the precaution, Mme. Adam tells us, of being inoculated against the plague.

The Theosophists of Madras were not simple-minded, but they could offer him no satisfying fare. " 'A heaven without a personal god, an immortality without a separate soul, purification without prayer.'

"This was the formula, the supreme conclusion, that filled the melancholy silence following on our conversation. A dark sadness brooded over the lonely house standing by the riverside amid strange trees and palms. 'Prayer' they said, 'Who is there to hear it? Each man has to face his own responsibility. You yourself are God. You must pray to yourself by means of your own actions.'

"A silence fell upon us, one of the saddest I have ever known. My last faint beliefs seemed to be falling from me, like falling leaves withered by the cold, calm reasoning of my instructors. One of these was a European who had come to India in search of the spiritual detachment of Buddha; the other was a Hindu, who though he disdained our western philosophies, had returned from Europe vested with our highest academical honours.

" 'You have told me,' I said, "' that our fading individuality persists for a little while after death. Can you give me absolute proof of this at least? "

" 'Yes,' he replied, 'we can prove it, but only by reasoning. Visible proofs, tangible proofs—no. To see those who are called the dead, special senses, special temperaments, and special circumstances are needful. But you may believe our words. We and many others worthy of credence have seen the departed, and written down accounts of what we have seen. Look in this bookcase.' "

"Was it for this that I had come to India?" wails the disappointed inquirer. "Brahminism tinctured with idolatry in the temples, and here a revised Positivism with the spiritualistic volumes to be obtained anywhere!" There were no more genuine fakirs even, he was told. For the performances of those in the past, he was again referred to the shelves.

He was told to go to Benares.

In the House of the Masters, he sat at the feet of Annie Besant. Her face in 1900 was still beautiful, though crowned with silver hair. "What must I do to join you?" he asked. He gives her answer thus: "Swear to regard all men as your equals and your brothers, meet them with the same love whether they be beggars or princes. Swear to seek spiritual truth by every means in your power. Those whom you left at Madras are tinged with Buddhism, from whose cold tenets your mystic temperament has recoiled. It is in esoteric Buddhism in its oldest form that we find our light and peace. We say that personal individuality is but a faint and ephemeral spark. To one so personal as you, this must sound a hard doctrine. Much of our belief is opposed to all the faiths in which you have been trained. Do not hate us if we pluck out those slumbering hopes which, perhaps unconsciously, sustain you."

To which Loti replies: "My hopes are dead. I have none to lose."

"Then come to us . . . ."

At the end of the book we read: "I have taken the simple oath required of me, and the Masters of the little House of Silence have made me one of their disciples." He is grateful to his teachers, but hardly pretends to have understood their teaching. "The little that I could tell might unbalance the mind, could lead perhaps to the terrors of the threshold, but no farther. The lonely little whitewashed house standing in its rose garden is the abode of renunciation and death. Peace reigns within it, but once you have entered, you can never be your old self again . . . . "*

This is but a literary flourish. Loti became his old self again, and that quickly. He had entered that house as so many others have done, at least in the spirit, and came out by that same door wherein he went. "Such evidence is brought before you that it is impossible to doubt the continuance of life beyond the grave." But this belief in immortality flickered out very soon. Loti did not find in India, any more than in Palestine, the guarantees of a future existence which he craved. Such hopes as the Hindu philosophies held out were of no use to him. To be merged in a divine, illimitable soul meant to so fierce an individualist, death by drowning. The only form of immortality acceptable to him was the survival of a Pierre Loti, rejuvenated, of course, who, in a glorified edition of this world, was to meet his dear, dead mother and Aziyade and all the women he had loved, and to go on loving and experiencing. Personality is built up on sensation. The immortality offered by most religions is the survival of something not one's self.

* Dr. Annie Besant under date June 11th, 1926, writes as follows: "I had the pleasure of seeing Pierre Loti in Benares, and found him a delightful conversationalist. What he stated in his book of his visit was quite accurate, and I have nothing to add to it."

PIERRE LOTI AS A NAVAL CAPTAIN.

CHAPTER XVII

LONELINESS IN PERSIA

LOTI left India in the spring of 1900, and made his way back to Europe through Persia. His route, of course, had been fixed beforehand, but, no doubt, he looked forward gladly to exchanging the rarefied atmosphere of Hinduism for the tougher and more palatable spiritual fare of Islam.

He must have sailed from Bombay or, less probably, from Calcutta, but he disdains to say a word about places on which the Anglo-Saxon has so emphatically placed his seal. His eyes were soon gladdened by the sight of a nominally independent Muslim capital—Muscat, "the town of the Imam, white and silent, wrapped in sunlight and in mystery, at the foot of a mass of rocks which resembled colossal carbonised sponges." It was, he found, very much the same as other Mohammedan cities, and roused in him the same emotions, though these must have begun to lose their keenness. Still, here was the Araby which "he adored, to which he longed always to return, though he had never been able exactly to understand by what charm it held him or to express its sad fascination." That mysterious fascination, he would have been disgusted to learn, was afterwards shared by the favourite novelists of the English *miss*.

After a friendly reception by the Imam, who, being a sovereign, had "charm", "ease" and an "aristocratic refinement", and who also loaded his distinguished visitor with costly arms and other presents, our traveller steamed across the gulf to Bushire. Here he collected a very modest caravan and, attended by a single French servant, started on his journey across Persia. "One's departure for the solitude and the unknown is always a solemn moment," he writes to Juliette Adam, on April 15th, "and so, by this last mail, I write to those I love." April, most Europeans find too late in the year for the Persian Gulf; but Loti braved the infernal heat in order to reach Ispahan during the rose season. He shows himself, in his account of the journey, a hardy, uncomplaining, and intrepid traveller. The man who never tired of denouncing European conveniences, had the grace to do without them himself without grumbling. His description of that eight days' climb to Shiraz is a vivid piece of word-painting. To his mind, the lonely, barren land presented a favourable contrast with India—with India, profaned and pillaged, where factory chimneys polluted the air, and the natives were driven to the works by energetic gentlemen in cork helmets and khaki suits! The calm of these Persian uplands soothed his soul. He paused to admire two Persian boys playing with their goats.

At Shiraz accommodation in a charming little, one-storeyed house, quite new and unfurnished, and surrounded by garden and a formidable wall, was found for him by Hajj-Abbas, the provost of the merchants. Later, he attended a reception given in his honour by this grave person, who had had his beard re-dipped in henna for the occasion, and, speaking Turkish, delighted Loti by abusing the perfidious English. The French man of letters paid a visit to the tombs of Hafiz and Sadi. Already there were roses all about in great profusion, but a sense almost of suffocation oppressed Loti, in spite of himself, as he wandered through the lanes of the walled labyrinthine city. The following passage comes unexpectedly from this fervent lover of the Orient:

"I tell myself again and again, 'I am at Shiraz,' and there is a certain charm in repeating that. A charm, yes, and also a certain distress; for this city, let it be confessed, while it remains a piece cut out of the past, is also one of the most inaccessible human communities. Here you experience that agony of utter strangeness, which must have been felt often enough by the travellers of old days, but which our posterity will one day not know at all. . . I ask myself, how would one get away from this place, whither could one flee, if one were assailed by a sudden longing, I won't say even for home, but for men of one's own sort and a more modern environment."

Well may M. Serban exclaim at this! Not unfairly he suggests that Loti was not sighing for a modern environment, which he had so often professed to loathe, but for a pair of green eyes like Aziyade's. The want of women's society was undoubtedly fidgeting our author. He was prepared to find the women of a Muslim country inaccessible, but not positively invisible like those of Persia. He saw black bundles moving on foot or on muleback, and these he knew were women. The tiniest girls alone went barefaced, and these, he noticed, had their hair dyed red. Determined to see what a Persian woman was like, he resorted to an ambush. On an adjoining roof his servant had noticed hanging out to dry a pair of green silk stockings and a pair of women's trousers. Loti set his servant to watch; but alas! the woman who at last appeared to "take down the washing" proved to be a toothless crone, probably a servant, who grinned unbecomingly at the Frank, no doubt enjoying his chagrin. After this disappointment, Loti positively revelled in the society of a Dutch bank manager and his wife, and dined with them, as I suspect, in the company of an English medical missionary! But travellers, we know, must be content.

From Shiraz he went on to Persepolis, and mused on the fall of emperors and empires without quoting Omar. On the road—if it could be called a road— he overtook a carriage which had broken down and was being drawn by the peasants. It contained, so he learnt, a woman of quality. He hardly disguises the eager curiosity with which he marked her daintily-shod foot protruding from her black envelope, and her elegant hands in pearl-grey gloves.

But he was to have no amorous adventures in Iran, though an adventure of a ruder sort awaited him on his entry into Ispahan. The people eyed the infidels with anger and scorn. At every inn the little caravan was turned away. A little man whispered to Loti that a friend of his had a house to let, at an exorbitant price. Loti was so tired that he was almost willing to buy the house for its weight in gold; but when the owner saw he had to deal with Christians he drove them away with maledictions. An old woman proved less fanatical and offered an apartment in her house. This was too much for the curious crowd, which in steadily increasing numbers had been following the strangers. They would not suffer infidels to defile the abode of a believer. The little party barricaded the door of their lodging and made ready to defend it, while Loti dispatched one of his men to seek help. This came in the form of tall Cossacks, who offered the hospitality of the Russian consulate in the name of their master, Prince Dabija. Thus was Loti delivered from the hands of the Ispahanis, who, with a change of mood not uncommon among mobs, helped to convey the foreigners' baggage to their refuge.

Zal-es-Sultan, the Shah's brother and the governor of the province, atoned in some measure for this discourteous reception. And though he realised by now the risks he was running, Loti made a supreme effort to penetrate the secret of the Persian woman. For a high price, he prevailed on a shoemaker to let him take a peep through a hole in his wall into some great man's garden. "And sure enough," he tells us, "three ladies were there, cutting flowers and filling baskets with them, no doubt in order to manufacture perfumes. I could have wished them prettier. I had been spoilt by the pictures on the antique boxes, and also by the peasant women surprised without their veils on the road. Very pale, a trifle too stout, these ladies had a certain charm, notwithstanding, and an air of primitive simplicity. Silk handkerchiefs, embroidered and bordered with sequins, enveloped their hair. They wore flounced vests, and above their trousers short flaring skirts like those of a ballet-girl. Everything seemed to be of silk, and the embroidery apparently dated from the time of Shah Abbas. These persons were guaranteed by my guide to belong to the highest rank of society."

Loti, it will be noticed, used his eyes well. His description of the Persian women does not differ materially from that of another witness, who, however, denounces their costume as indecent and uncomfortable, says they dye their hair red, raddle their faces with paint, and lose their figures hopelessly upon maternity. So the devotee of Aziyade was probably spared a rude shock by the strict application of the Mohammedan rule.

At Teheran he found other company which he always appreciated. He was shown over the Shah's palace by an exceedingly elegant prince, and was affectionately and graciously greeted by the court cat, a large Angora, which he found, delightfully enough, seated on the throne of Persia. (He apologises for the inevitable pun—*un chat sur le trône du Chah*). In the absence of the sovereign, the eminent Frenchman was entertained to dinner by the Vizier; but so far from resembling a scene from the Arabian Nights, the function was on the lines of Paris or London.

Loti made his way over the Elburz mountains to the Caspian, and went home through Circassia and across the Black Sea. His visit to Persia resulted in a very good book, but it was a personal disappointment. "Never yet," he complains, "in the House of Islam, have I felt myself so much a stranger and so much alone."

CHAPTER XVIII

AT LAST—ANGKOR!

THE Boxer outbreak in China recalled Loti to the East before he could have passed much more than a month at home. He had been promoted *capitaine de frégate*, in 1898, and sailed now from Cherbourg on August 2nd, 1900, as first aide-de-camp to Vice-Admiral Pottier, the commander of the French naval forces taking part in the allied demonstration against China.

It was Loti's fate to arrive on every theatre of war when hostilities had practically terminated. But the banks of the Pei-ho were still strewn thickly with corpses as he went up to Peking on a mission to General Voyron. He recites with proper enthusiasm the story of the gallant defence of the French legation by Frenchmen—he is loath to acknowledge the help rendered by the British and other allies, or to ascribe to them any good intentions. The memory of Chinese cruelty and treachery seemed to fade away so soon as he observed the ruined pillaged palaces of Chinese royalty; though respect for fallen majesty did not prevent him from establishing himself in a palace once inhabited by the Empress. The room was extraordinarily cold and uncomfortable.

He slept on an imperial bed in carved ebony, on a mattress of precious silk, but over his freezing anatomy he had to draw a soldier's blanket. For his study he used another of the imperial apartments, and here one day he was disturbed by a white and yellow cat, "elegant and distinguished, with the air of a grand seigneur." Probably one of the Empress's favourites. This courtier regarded him at first with natural suspicion, but Loti knew all about cats and the etiquette they demand, and very soon friendly relations were established. The intruder provided puss with meals, and she sat by him while he worked. The present writer has noticed that while dogs acquire the manner of the men with whom they live, there is but one code of feline manners and ethics. Only where cats live under a persecution, as in Spain, do they fail to recognise the conventional courtesies or to make the same response. A dog is an English dog, or a French dog, as the case may be; but a cat is a cat all the world over.

And as such was dear to Loti.

With the connivance of the Japanese guard, he and other allied officers penetrated even into the bed-chamber of the Son of Heaven. He speculates on the mentality of that mysterious being and pictures his distress and bewilderment on finding himself thrown into the world of common men.

At the women of China the author glanced with an expert's eye merely, one suspects, out of force of habit. He had rounded his half-century, had known and kissed so many women, women more or less of every nation! In search, perhaps, of a new sensation, or to quicken his imagination, he dosed himself with the finest Chinese opium, and dressing himself in gorgeous robes, stolen no doubt from the imperial wardrobe, lay back on his divan. Under the influence of the drug, he discovered beauty and symmetry in the bizarre decorations of the palace, he became possessed of a Chinese soul, and surveyed time and space with infinite complacency. We have sometimes been told that a man becomes what he eats—Loti's experience suggests that taste in art might be similarly acquired or directed. Perhaps the humour of Artemus Ward might be better appreciated upon a diet of pea-nuts, and the charm of certain Italian primitives be heightened after a course of garlic and gnocchi.

Loti visited what we may call the loggia of Confucius, and particularly directed the attention of the new literary generation of France to the sage's prediction: "The new literature will be the literature of pity." Alas! a generation has passed since Loti saw that inscription in Chinese characters, and literature, so far from stimulating pity, tends to disclaim all ethical purpose, and to concentrate on the mere photography of mind and events.

Li-Hung-Chang, that famous celestial statesman, who was to die two or three months later, granted an interview to the French officer as a distinguished man of letters. Li made a great show of poverty and abandonment, but this did not deceive the visitor. The conversation proceeded much on the same lines as with Lord Curzon and Marschall von Bieberstein, as recorded in their memoirs, the

Chinese statesman beginning by inquiring how old Loti was, how much money he had, and whether his venerable parents were living. Asked whether he had any children, the Frenchman was able to return a more satisfactory answer than Lord Curzon, who on admitting that, though he was thirty he had not got any, was floored by the question: "What have you been doing then all this time?"

At Peking, our author met the brave and adventurous Colonel Marchand, who had contested the possession of Fashoda with Kitchener only two years before. The sight of him helped to arouse Loti's bitterness against the English. The scarlet of our troops, he picturesquely remarks, was reflected like blood on the waters of a lake near by. The thought of the Boers, he tells Juliette Adam, keeps him awake at night. Hearing of the death of Queen Victoria, he speaks of us as "the people of prey." In fact, whenever he alludes to "atrocities committed by a nation he will not name," one suspects that he means the British. He deplores the looting of the palaces; but in his house at Rochefort are to be seen a number of objects which are credibly asserted to have been imperial property. Inviting Mme. Adam to a *fête chinoise* at his home in 1903, he promises that she shall sit on a real Chinese throne, not, he told Mme. Barthou, the throne of state, but a throne used by the Empress all the same. Presumably it was not sold to him by the Wielder of the Vermilion Pencil.*

* Claude Farrère compliments Loti on having secured this, and other precious objects, which the dreadful Germans would have preferred to destroy.

Loti stayed long enough in the imperial capital to witness the restoration of Chinese authority and the celebration of the Allies' triumph. In a torchlight procession, German soldiers linked arms with French bluejackets and chanted the *Marseillaise*—a spectacle not wholly pleasing to our author, who seems to have thought the Europeans would have been better employed fighting each other than against Asiatics. A banquet and a ball took place in the halls of the ineffably sacred palace. Loti's sense of the impiety of this was, he fancies, shared by the lady who led the cotillon, for, not liking the stare of those strange Chinese figures on the wall, she danced out into the open, drawing the dancers after her.

"Peking," concludes Loti with manifest regret," "is finished, its prestige gone, its mystery dispelled. And this imperial city was one of the last refuges of the unknown and the marvellous, one of the last bulwarks of an ancient civilization, incomprehensible and legendary."

He predicted the eclipse of another ancient empire, that of Korea, which he set foot in while in the Far East. The officers of the *Redoutable* visited Seoul and were entertained to a banquet by the Emperor. This potentate had "a face of pale parchment, a smiling expression, keen lively eyes," and that air of distinction which Loti never failed to find in royalty.

Leaving Taku on June 15th, 1901, the *Redoutable*, Loti aboard, cruised the rest of the summer and autumn in Japanese waters. Loti, we know, had quitted Japan sixteen years before, without the least regret. Now the petty, pretty artificiality of its life contrasted agreeably with the tragic gloom of Peking. *La Troisième Jeunesse de Madame Prune* is written, therefore, more sympathetically than *Madame Chrysanthème.* Loti had by now learned to take his emotions, as far as women were concerned, at their proper value. In Japan, moreover, he did not seek emotion but amusement. He called first on his old friends, and learnt that his former "wife," Okane-San, was now married for life to a respectable lantern manufacturer. With a very proper delicacy, he refrained from calling upon her. He found it enjoyable, now, to sit on black, velvet cushions in empty, white rooms while little Japanese damsels, irresistibly reminding him of little cats, danced and made music for his sole pleasure. With his curious flair for things funereal, he lighted on a tea-shop specially affected by the coffin-bearers and watched them carrying their gruesome burdens.

It was, indeed, to an old burial-ground, attached to a little temple, that his tenderest memories of Japan clung. There he used to meet and talk with the young daughter of the bonze, a simpler, more sympathetic creature than any he had so far encountered in this land. There was nothing sensual in their acquaintance; he wondered himself what they found in each other. "Mousmé, who had not the eyes of a mousmé, pretty enigmatical flower, blossom of the pagoda and the graveyard, how much of her did I understand, how much of me has she understood?" For he knew no more of her language than sufficed for a traveller's needs. The last farewells were exchanged with a certain emotion. For the first time, he kissed her, and she made a shy effort to return the salute as though she had never kissed before—and almost certainly, being a Japanese, she had not. So the episode concludes with a faint echo of the old refrain. He plucked some flowers to remind him of her, just to conform to his old habits, but well knowing, this time, that he would throw them away—"like those others culled at such moments of farewell, when he believed with the credulity of youth that he would cherish them for ever."

He confesses to leaving Japan with a shade more of regret and tenderness than after his former visit. The better side of the people's nature has been revealed to him, and then—he knows that this is good-bye for ever.

Loti had resigned himself to a stay of two years in Eastern waters, but his ship was unexpectedly ordered to return to Indo-China. Leaving Nagasaki on October 30th, Touran was reached six days later, and Saigon on November 19th, 1901.

Saigon—"a colonial town which smells of musk and opium. A damp heat weighs on one's chest. The air is like the vapour of a cauldron. Saigon— a town the very name of which used to have a sinister sound for me, reminding me, as it did, that here my brother absorbed the germs of death. But it has long since been familiar to me, this town of exile and languor. Why, I hardly dislike it now. It has even its memories. I have almost loved here, certainly I have suffered much. . . ."

Loti was recalling, doubtless, his call here when he was being sent back to France, in 1883, in what he believed to be disgrace. Now, a captain, A.D.C. to the Admiral, an officer of the Legion of Honour, and a member of the Academy, he could ask what favours he liked of his superiors. He sought and obtained leave for twenty days, to visit the temples of Angkor.

This pilgrimage must have been long contemplated by Pierre Loti; contemplated uncertainly at least as early as his entry into the navy. Roaming the world, he must often have thought of that temple in the recesses of Asia, pictured by him as a child in the upper room at Rochefort. Across the oceans, those towers beckoned. In the heart of many a man, there is also an Angkor, a peculiar spot hallowed by memory, to which he tells himself he must return some day . . . But it was not with an old love that Loti had a tryst to keep this time. He was following the path pointed out to him across the wide intervening years by his early, oh, such a very early, self.

But it was, I imagine, with a certain reluctance that he made his preparations for the journey. Here was an admission that it could not be put off any longer, that he was nearing the moment foreseen by him thirty-five years before. And so, on November 23rd, 1901, he set out from Saigon.

The Governor-General of Indo-China, his friend, Paul Doumer, had seen to it that no obstacle should bar his path. By railway and steamer he proceeded to Pnom-Penh, the decaying capital of Cambodia.

Thence he went up the river to a point within Siamese territory, where a train of bullock carts—the carts resembling mandolines—had been held in readiness for him. So on through dense forests, he travelled, till, through a clearing, suddenly he perceived in the distance a tiara of tall grey towers. . . .

"Oh, I knew them at once!" he exclaims, "I saw them in the picture which moved me so much, years ago, in my boyhood's 'museum.' At last then I behold it, the mysterious Angkor!"

"Yet . . . I'm hardly stirred as much as I expected. It is too late in life, and I have seen so many remains of the storied past, too many temples, too many palaces, too many ruins. For that matter, one can't see well in the dazzling light. And noon approaches, compelling us to sleep."

With curiosity he examines these majestic monuments of a forgotten civilisation, as though wondering why their very name should have exercised so powerful a spell over that well-remembered boy. He penetrates to the very heart of the vast enclosure. "Here then is the sanctuary which haunted my childish imagination, the sanctuary to which I have come after so many wanderings, when night begins to fall over my vagrant life. If offers me but a dismal welcome! I didn't anticipate these torrents of rain, this enforced seclusion among the spider's webs, this hour's solitude surrounded by phantom-gods." Things turn out so differently. . . Patiently and with understanding, he explores the ruins, leaving us an eloquent and detailed description

ANGKOR.

of a place which he felt merited a more enthusiastic study.

And then—he took the road to the coast, home. "I turned to take a last look . . . This pilgrimage which I promised myself in my boyhood, was at last accomplished. Already it belonged to the past, as to-morrow, my whole life would belong. I shall never again see those tall strange towers rising into the sky. Even as I looked, the forest shut them out of sight."

To some it may seem fantastic that a man should imagine a link between himself and a spot where he had never been before, thousands of miles away from his birthplace. But sentiment throws its tentacles in strange directions, and these may trip you up very far afield, and at very unlikely moments. The first sight of Lisbon may recall a picture that hung in a dimly-remembered room, in a very different country, and that may evoke other pictures, other faces, other times. On this sentimental journey, Loti appears less sentimental than in most of his works. Rather, the sentiment is absolutely genuine. It is the regret which all humanity feels for its irrecoverable youth, the half-pitying respect with which we regard our dead childish selves. There are no passages of love or lust in *Pèlerin d'Angkor*—with a dignified gesture, of which, unhappily, he was not always capable, the man brushes all that aside, as something not quite becoming his years. Some who have not liked him at all so far, will feel a new sympathy with Pierre Loti, reading of his journey into the forests of Siam.

CHAPTER XIX

ENCHANTED BY THE DISENCHANTED

Loti landed in France in March, 1902, and, on April 8th, was granted three months sick leave. At the end of that period he was appointed A.D.C. to the Maritime Prefect of Rochefort. He had plenty of literary work to occupy him. According to the careful bibliography prepared by M. Serban, *Les Derniers Jours de Pékin* (evidently written on the spot and aboard the *Redoutable*) appeared in the February of this year; his article on Muscat in the *Revue des Deux Mondes* in March, his articles on India, under the title of *Dans l'Inde Affamée*, in the same journal in January and February, 1903, to be re-published under the title of *L'Inde Sans les Anglais*, by Calmann-Levy, the next month. *Vers Ispahan* appeared twelve months after, and *La Troisième Jeunesse de Madame Prune* in 1905.

In July, 1902, took place the marriage of his grand-niece, Mademoiselle Duvignau. (Loti's sister, Mme. Bon, it must not be forgotten, was his senior by nearly twenty years). On this occasion, as frequently, he invited Juliette Adam to Hendaye. As passion waned, and since the loss of his mother, his love for "his second mother" grew warmer and more insistent. He is always begging her to visit him, reminding her that the garden at Hendaye, which she had made herself responsible for, is going to wrack and ruin. These middle-aged friends could appreciate the most schoolboyish of jokes. One night, in the course of a visit, Mme. Adam was awakened by what seemed to be the movement of a cat—a visitor always to be expected in Loti's household—crawling across the bed cover. But it seemed to be a spectral cat, for, on striking a light, nothing was to be seen. Outside, however, was to be heard smothered laughter, which the lady smothered very effectively by emptying a jugful of water over the conspirators. Loti confessed afterwards that he had been teasing his guest by means of a plummet and line let down through a hole he had made in her ceiling.

One of the jokers was Mustafa Kamil, then and afterwards, a warm friend of Loti's. This man was famous in his day as the leader of the Egyptian nationalists, and to him our author's peculiar animosity against the British may be in some measure attributed. Mustafa, who died five or six years later, was a slightly-built man, of fair complexion, only to be distinguished from an European by his tarbush.* Even Juliette Adam allowed herself to be infected with his prejudices, and speaks of Kitchener as having rendered himself notorious by his severity in the Sudan.

* I met this man in London several times in 1906. He offered me a post on the staff of a paper he was founding at Cairo, which his violently anti-British policy made it impossible for me to accept, though the barbarous executions of Denshawi had very much swayed my sympathies towards the Egyptians just then.—E.B.d'A.

Loti's pro-Turkish sentiments were universally known by this time, even in Government circles, to which knowledge of this kind penetrates but slowly. The Germans were steadily courting the favour of the Turks, and it occurred to someone that the famous author of *Aziyade* might help to improve Turkish relations with France. On September 10th, 1903, he was appointed to the command of the *Vautour*, the gunboat which France maintained off Constantinople.

That brilliant novelist known to us as Claude Farrère was serving on the *Vautour* at this time, and has left us some delightful thumb-nail sketches of Loti in his role of commander.* It is a pitch-dark night in the Aegean, somewhere off the coast of Asia Minor. The captain has been humming Lalo's *Roi d'Ys* steadily for two hours. Farrère discovers land and reports accordingly. "Cape Sigri so many points to starboard, sir." Loti considers his lieutenant with a lack-lustre eye, goes on humming, then meditatively strolls across, takes a look at the chart, and gives an order in an indifferent voice. He goes on humming. Some time passes. At the risk of a rebuke, Farrère makes so bold as to ask, "Are you particularly fond of Lalo, sir?" "Of Lalo? Not that I know of. Why?" "Only, sir, that you have been humming his *Roi d'Ys* for over two hours now." Loti laughs outright. "The deuce I have! I was quite unaware of it. I was thinking." "And what the deuce could he have been thinking about?" speculates the young officer.

* *Revue critique*, July, 1923.

At Constantinople, Loti goes ashore to celebrate Christmas Eve, possibly with M. Constans, the French ambassador, at Pera. The officers make merry in his absence. They send an invitation to Mademoiselle Balkis, the captain's cat, to join them at supper (the traditional *réveillon*). Now, the officers of the *Vautour* had their own cat, and two exquisite dishes were prepared, consisting of turkey, meat, and a peculiarly delicious dish only found in the Bosporus. How different was the behaviour of the two cats! The ward-room cat, though already gorged to repletion, fell upon these delicacies like one famished; whereas Mademoiselle Balkis, "grave, discreet, almost royal in her manner," though she had no appetite, made a point of eating perhaps a third of the dishful, out of simple courtesy to her hosts, and leaving the rest, retired, graceful and purring, to her own quarters.

We suspect Farrère and his shipmates of being responsible for the solemn baptism of Mademoiselle Balkis, which, it was reported in the French press, took place on the guardship in presence of a distinguished gathering. But Loti sanctioned the elaborate tomfoolery which shocked religious opinion in France, and on the other hand, absurdly enough, convinced the rationalists that he was a fanatical Christian. During a part of this time Loti had the company of his wife and their fifteen-year old boy. His old friend, Sarah Bernhardt, also paid a visit to Constantinople. Nevertheless, he again fell to the fatal fascination of the yashmak. An elaborate practical joke was played on him. Its immediate result was the novel, *Les Désenchantées*. This work, which I find rather dull, and abounding in repetitions, is a relation of the author's friendly and sentimental intercourse with three Turkish ladies whom he calls Djenane, Zeyneb, and Melek. They are very different types from the Circassian odalisque— women of high rank, educated in European fashion, but far above the European standard. They enlist Loti's sympathies on behalf of themselves and their sisters, chafing, in spite of their culture and understanding, under the restrictions imposed by Muslim law and custom, unable, for instance, to go out unveiled or to have any male friend other than a husband, father, or brother. Loti, a high old Tory, hears with suspicion such words as progress and emancipation. He defends the men of Turkey against their strictures; but, in the end, he is won over by their personal charm rather than by their arguments, and writes this book to let the world know what the women of the new Turkey are feeling and suffering behind the harem lattices. Djenane is the heroine. She dies, of course, after his departure from Stambul. The author's account of his sensations upon leaving the city bears, it must be admitted, a strong resemblance to the concluding passages of *Aziyade* already quoted.

To the day of his death, Loti believed in Djenane and believed her to be dead. It was not till he was buried that a French woman of letters, styling herself Marc Hélys, startled the literary world by announcing that she was the heroine of *Les Désenchantées*, and that the episodes described in the novel were deliberately contrived by her.

Her version is given at unnecessary length in her book, *L'Envers d'un Roman*, published by Perrin in 1923.

Marc Hélys had spent a good deal of time in Turkey and spoke the language fluently. Returning to Constantinople in April, 1904, she found the Ottoman ladies very much excited about Loti. The author of *Aziyade* had become the object of a cult. Everyone knew his name and knew of his attachment to their country. Great was the demand for his books at the library at the Tunnel Station. But Loti of the twentieth century was no longer the sub-lieutenant who had pierced the veil of the harem, and sought the friendship of watermen and porters at the beginning of Abd-ul-Hamid's reign. He led, on the contrary, "a notably retired life aboard his ship. He was seen very little. He understood how to enfold himself in an air of mystery and to appear inaccessible. The Sultan was said to be more easily approached than he."

In the fashionable quarter of Taxim lived a great friend of Marc Hélys, a married woman named Zennur. She and her sister, Nurye, had been educated in Western style, and were, in fact, the granddaughters of a Frenchman. On the mother's side they were of Circassian race. Their father boasted that there was not a drop of Osmanli blood in their veins. Zennur's house was furnished in the French manner; within its walls she appeared to live as a Frenchwoman; but she wore the veil, and was bound, as regarded her intercourse with the outer world, by the hard-and-fast conventions taken by

ignorant Muslims to be a part of their religion.*
(As the social conventions are regarded by most
Christians, too, it is only fair to say).

Zennur had written to Loti at Rochefort, two
years before, telling him how much she appreciated
his books. She and her French friend had now the
bright idea of writing again to him, aboard the
Vautour, asking him to meet them. His reply,
courteously and cautiously worded, seemed to
contain some suspicion that a trick was being played
on him. However, curiosity got the better of him,
and alighting, heavily veiled from their carriage, at
the appointed spot on the waterside at Therapia, they
found him seated on a bench, accompanied by one
of his officers, waiting for them. His manner was, as
usual, awkward and hesitating. He pointed out
that they had him at a great disadvantage and asked
them to unveil. This they declared to be impossible,
and he never repeated the request. He was surprised,
we are told, to find three Turkish women speaking
French so well, but the fluency in Turkish of at least two
of them disarmed his suspicions. Marc Hélys gave
her name as Leyla, which in the book he alters into
the harsher-sounding Djenane. The other two called
themselves Zeyneb and Nurye. They walked up and
down the road, talking about his books, questioning
him about his adventures and love-affairs. "Leyla"
twitted him with having scattered fragments of his

* I visited Constantinople two years later. On the steamer was a Turkish lady,
the wife of a Pasha, just the kind of woman described. She dined in the saloon,
even discarding the veil, and spoke freely and gaily in French with the women
passengers of all nationalities, but I never heard her exchange a word with a man
except an attendant, who seemed to be keeping close watch on her, and was no
doubt under pledge to report her doings to her husband.—E.B. d'A.

heart all about the world. He could not have much of it left. "He protested. He had left nothing in Japan, very little in Oceania. (Poor Rarahu). It was in Turkey that the greater part remained."

"Two-thirds?" inquired Nurye.

"More, perhaps three-quarters," was the reply.

The conversation was poor, and Loti knew it. For all the adulation he had received in the Avenue Friedland and the like quarters, he had not forgotten the impression produced on the Queen of Rumania's ladies, and he remained deeply conscious of his own insufficiency. As the three veiled women took their departure, "Loti bared his head. We saw him flush to the roots of his hair, his lips trembled, and his hands also. He stood there speechless, in his eyes a kind of entreaty which he could not articulate. Profoundly touched by his emotion, we offered him our hands, over which he bent respectfully."

This unexpectedly humble, wistful attitude corrected the young women's first unfavourable impression. They resolved to continue the acquaintance and to make themselves the heroines of another of his romances. Between the first and second meetings, oddly enough, Loti was entertained by the Turkish women's father, a person of considerable consequence. The ladies, separated from the men guests, of course, were assembled in another room, behind the curtains, whence they took peeps at their all-unsuspecting friend, even making music for his entertainment.

Thus began, half in jest, the acquaintance which, almost exactly as it proceeded, is chronicled in the novel. The name Djenane was borrowed from the owner of the house in which some of the meetings took place—a woman whose life afforded certain parallels with that of Aziyade. In Loti's cabin the three ladies were astonished to perceive a lugubrious object, the turbeh or headstone of Aziyade, which he had had removed and replaced. Nurye read out the name "Hadidje Kalkassi," and claimed Loti's lost love as a remote kinswoman. Later they went to see her grave at Eyub. On a previous visit they had to leave precipitately, as some soldiers had seen them conversing with a man, and were approaching to recall them to a sense of propriety! One cannot imagine the English soldier regarding himself as the custodian of the sex conventions.

Marc Hélys wrote to Loti, confessing that they had sought to know him, in the first instance more or less by way of a prank; but she continued: "We shall never forget you. We shall never forget you because, thanks to you, we have tasted what should be the delight of your western women—intellectual contact with a superior mind, and a part, however modest and fugitive, in the thoughts of a man like you. You haven't seen our faces, you don't know whether we are pretty or ugly as witches, yet you bestow on us an affectionate sympathy."

Many men, it may be safely asserted, who would sneer at Loti's voluptuousness, would not have troubled themselves so far. No doubt, Marc felt a little mean. The worst of it was that it was she whom he seemed to prefer, though he succeeded in seeing the other two without their veils, and traced a likeness between Zennur and his dead love. Marc found herself obliged to return to Paris. To explain her absence, and in order, as I imagine, to secure for herself a lasting place in Loti's memory, she contrived to make out that she was going to Smyrna to marry a man she did not love. In the end, she wrote announcing that she was in the act of taking poison— and Loti believed it.

Marc Hélys is to be left to the judgment of her readers. She might, at least, have devised some other means of escape from her difficult situation than by harrowing the man's feelings and leaving a tragic memory behind. But Marc Hélys is, I understand, a journalist, and delicacy is rather an embarrassment than an asset in her profession. That Constans, the French ambassador, should have been privy to the fraud practised on one of his official colleagues, as she alleges, comes also as a shock. She has the grace to confess that she felt particularly guilty as regards Loti's wife, from whom she had received, as "Leyla," some long and sympathetic letters.

Otherwise considered, the conspiracy seems innocent enough, and hardly amounted to a deception. For Zennur and Nurye were what they represented themselves to be, and their case hardly differed from that stated in the novel. Marc Hélys has perhaps the right to be thanked for her share in producing a book which went into 220,000 copies, and which did direct attention to the painful condition of the women of Turkey.

As to Zennur and Nurye, they narrowly escaped turning a comedy into a tragedy. For reasons not divulged, they fled (so Marc Hélys tells us) to Belgrade, where the Ottoman Government made ineffective demands for their extradition. From Serbia, they went to France. One ultimately married and settled down in "Europe," the other returned at last to her own country. From Loti they received, the same informant tells us, assistance, both materially and socially, even visiting him at Rochefort. Zennur, at least, was in Paris as late as December 21st, 1909, the eve of the reception of Loti's friend, Jean Aicard, into the Academy as successor to François Coppée. On that date there appears a long article by her in the *Figaro*, vigorously replying to the violent criticisms of which *Les Désenchantées* had been the subject. She affirms the accuracy of the whole story, declares herself to be "Zeyneb," and Djenane, "her Circassian friend," to be dead. As to Loti's assailants, she tears them to pieces. One of them, she points out, bases his knowledge of Turkish women on his acquaintance with Tunis—another on her experiences in Egypt; while a third unfortunate, masquerading as a Mussulman, under the name of Sefer Bey, she proves to be a mere Levantine, a man of Pera, a miserable Armenian, whose knowledge of Constantinople was confined to the Grande Rue de Pera. This letter she signs as Hadidje Zennur, daughter of Nury Bey, grand-daughter of Rechad Bey, Comte de Chateauneuf. In consequnece of this exposure, I should not be surprised to learn that the wretched Levantine adopted yet another disguise! His Turkish friend had indeed made Loti's enemies his footstool when he appeared next day among the immortals to pronounce a speech of welcome to his nominee.*

Five years later, Marc Hélys was present at a *conférence* in the Salle de la Vie Féminine, when Madame Bartet read aloud "Djenane's" farewell letter, while Loti covered his face with his hands. I hope she felt ashamed of herself.

There is, I should add, a passage in a later work of Loti's (*Suprêmes Visions d'Orient*) which makes this affair of the *Désenchantées* "curiouser and curiouser." The hero, re-visiting Constantinople in 1910, refers to her who in a measure had been the re-incarnation of Aziyade—who had come even from the same village. For Leyla, like the other two, had claimed Circassian lineage. With the usual difficulties he traced another Turkish lady who had been privy to his clandestine acquaintance, and knew all three. On finding herself face to face

* Arthur Lynch, who spent three months in Constantinople some time before 1900, writes: "I once had the good fortune to meet with one of Pierre Loti's *désenchantées*. She was the daughter of Nouri Bey, a remarkable man, who was himself the grandson of a French general. He had been brought up in the Sultan's palace—*nourri dans le sérail*—and at the time I knew him was virtually, if not nominally, minister of foreign affairs.

"Nouri Bey had inherited the wit of his Gallic ancestors, and his conversation was vivacious and sparkling. One day, he told me of the accomplishments of his daughter, who was then some twelve years of age. She used to read the *Times* and *Figaro* and mark in pencil any paragraph to which his attention should be drawn. Sometimes she would write a précis of the matter. He asked me to call on the following morning.

"I was kept waiting some time in a little plainly-furnished ante-room. The door opened, then mademoiselle appeared, then drew back as if she had not known there was anyone there. She had no veil, and her clothes, except for the flash of yellow and red of her blouse and short skirt, looked like badly-made English garments, full at the waist. I could have easily believed she was sixteen.

"Her face was the great attraction. Not at all of the intellectual type, still less of the strained and overworn *féministe*. She looked a jolly little wench with her black hair pulled straight back on a round forehead surmounting a round face of ruddy apple hue. Apple-faced was the epithet that came irresistibly into my mind, and she made me think of Devonshire—but for her eastern eyes, large but not fully opened, dark, laughing, frank, yet with all the guile of the gardens of Gul. Then she opened her mouth—a full red mouth displaying a row of white even teeth—and said in a delightful broken English accent, 'My fader attend you. You will find him above.' I bowed, and my delightful little Turkish vision vanished."

with him, she exclaimed at once, "Tell me all you know."

"I?" said Loti astonished. "But it is for you to speak. Tell me, where is her tomb?"

The Turkish lady: "But I don't know, I swear it. I left Stambul before——before the end of the drama. And the others have not written to me. If you only knew in what complete mystery these things are hidden in this country."

And so the interview ended, leaving us as perplexed as Loti himself. Was the Turkish lady in the secret? Was her emotion a pretence? Had Marc Hélys imposed on her also?—but this seems almost impossible. Or was Loti, at the age of sixty, simply recalling his readers' attention to that last love affair, and inventing just the kind of sequel they had a right to expect?

There are plenty of men capable of acting generously towards women who would not bestir themselves to help another man. Loti was not, as we have seen, one of these. While pursuing his adventure with the three *hanums*, he writes to Juliette Adam: "I am in disgrace with your friend the Sultan, because I helped Jellaleddin Pasha* to escape to Corfu. But don't talk about it. He suspects me, but is not sure about it."

But Abd-ul-Hamid bore him no grudge, and seated him by his side at a banquet. This was the third occasion when our author drank beyond his measure. Loti is one of the few writers who have attempted to present the clever but unfortunate Commander

* Probably Jamal al Din, a Turkish man of letters.

of the Faithful under a sympathetic guise. Readers of *Désenchantées* should remember that scene where "Zahide," seeking a divorce, is surprised in the harem of the palace by the Sultan himself:

"He who stood on the threshold was the man least comprehensible by the western world—the Khalifa, a man of superhuman responsibilities, who holds vast Islam in his hand, and must defend it, not only against the surreptitious coalition of the Christian nations, but also against the devastating march of time—he who is known in the most inaccessible deserts of Asia as the Shadow of God.

"Coming now to pay his respects to his venerated mother, he perceived the anguish and entreaty in the expression of the young woman kneeling before him. And her look penetrated that mysterious heart, which hardens sometimes under the weight of his pontificate, but which throbs with a personal and exquisite pity, unknown to all."

One hopes that was so. Another aspect of Abd-ul-Hamid is given us by Loti writing after his fall: "He was seen nowhere, and was felt everywhere. Under the pressure of his omnipresence, Stambul trembled. He never issued from his retreat at Yildiz, yet, by thousands of ears, he heard. Not the merest trifle escaped his knowledge—he knew even what I was doing, and took the trouble to make my likeness known to his agents, by whom I was watched, though with consideration, and even with a view to my own protection."*

* *Suprêmes Visions d'Orient.*

Except against possible jealous husbands, these precautions must have been unnecessary. Loti during this, his third visit to Constantinople, endeared himself to the Turks, to whom he was an unofficial ambassador, and to the men under his command. When, on March 24th, 1905, the *Phrygie* came to take him away, the crew of the *Vautour* cheered him to the echo. The quays of Galata were lined with Turks come to do honour to this good friend of Islam. One hopes the dogs of Constantinople, so near their doom, also signified their appreciation of this staunch champion. It was a sad day in the harems. At the moment of his departure, the love of Aziyade and Djenane caught sight of a closed carriage passing very slowly along the quay—and through the window he glimpsed, for the briefest moment, a raised veil and two black eyes which spoke the women of Turkey's farewell.

CHAPTER XX

LOTI visited Egypt in 1907, at the invitation of the Khedive, Abbas Hilmi, to whom he seems to have been presented at Constantinople; an invitation which had no doubt been procured by his friend Mustafa Kamil. That astute and patriotic Egyptian had noted the beginnings of the Entente Cordiale, had conceived it to be prejudicial to the interests of his country. The year before, had occurred the Tabah incident, when Egyptians in the cafés of Cairo stood up and encored the Turkish national anthem. I have no doubt that Kamil determined, at this critical moment, to exploit Loti's extravagant Muslim sympathies in favour of his own land, and to the disadvantage of its British rulers.

Loti certainly did his best in this direction. The sight of Modern Egypt was, indeed, well calculated to arouse all his pet prejudices, as Mustafa well knew. Islam in subjection—the English in authority —modern civilisation overspreading and adapting the remains of an august antiquity—these considerations might have urged our author to express himself even more intemperately than in *La Mort de Philae*. But his partialities spoil the book.

I suspect that Mustafa, was ever at his elbow, distracting his attention from the scenery and the monuments to some fresh evidence of Anglo-Saxon guile. The Egyptian, of course, wanted a pamphlet on behalf of his countrymen—he was not concerned to inspire a real work of literature.

And as a pamphlet, Loti's Egypt cannot be considered convincing or arresting. He could feel, but could not think; could talk, but could not argue. He did not understand the ultimate aims of the people who were using him. When he lamented the introduction of railways into the country and the development of industry, Mustafa Kamil must have smiled. It was not his ambition, I can say it, my hand on my heart, to restore Egypt to its Pharaonic conditions.

But it was Mustafa, I am sure, who got Loti to describe Mehemet Ali as "a prince adventurous and chivalrous as some legendary hero, and withal one of the greatest sovereigns of modern history!" (Perhaps Loti did not know that he waged war on his master, the Khalifa, and dealt a deadly blow at the prestige of the Sultan). When, too, our traveller is shocked at the irreverent behaviour of tourists in the mosques, one can but recall the behaviour of the French in their own churches. Over and over again, in fact, one is tempted to shut the book and to tell Pierre Loti that he does not know what he is talking about.

And nowadays, which, of course, is not his fault, we have become so used to the traveller's sneer at other travellers! Every Oxford undergraduate making his first trip abroad tells us about the funny

English people he sees at his hotel. Loti, being able to afford a dahabiyeh, and travelling under Khedivial patronage, was well placed to make fun of less fortunate people who had to journey by excursion steamer, and to avail themselves of the facilities offered by the abhorred Thomas Cook and Son. The playful gambols of drunken French sailors,* often sympathetically related by him, were, we are to suppose, much less offensive to Mohammedan ideas of decorum than the visits of "Cookistes." It is the feminine variety of British tourist, by the way, which goads him into ironic fury. He found them ugly and ungainly. That our prettiest and most charming women find they can pass their time more pleasantly at home than roaming eternally from one foreign hotel to another, is perhaps true, and may explain, in a measure, this unfavourable opinion; but there is also this to it—you have to get used to the looks of a people before you can appreciate them. I have met Dutchmen who honestly held their women folk to be more beautiful than ours. Many Britons visiting Italy for the first time can see no beauty in Italian women; in a Belgian paper not long ago, a leader-writer reflected with satisfaction that God had punished the abominable English by giving them such ugly wives.† Probably a fair number of countrywomen staying that year at Luxor were definitely pretty; but Loti could not see it.

* See *Les Trois Dames de le Kasbah.*
† This may sound incredible to the simple English folk who poured out their sympathy on "gallant little Belgium." But I read the passage in a Brussels paper while staying at Ostende in Sept., 1923.—E.B. d'A.

Enjoying, as I have said, privileges denied to the average tourist, he visited the museum of Cairo by night in search of sensations. For a life beyond the grave he had ceased to hope; from the wisdom of the Egyptians he expected no enlightenment. The mummied dead he discovered to be very dead indeed and some of them badly preserved at that. . . . Some of the details are of the nastiest. It is curious how this man, who could not endure the thought of his own death, revelled in mortuary spectacles and reflections.

That taste admittedly entitles him to speak with understanding of the Pharaohs. Otherwise, he brought no learning or real critical faculty to their ancient seats. His admiration was as indiscriminate, and his awe as naïf, as that of any Cookiste, or close-cropped German who could only murmur "*wunderschön!*" For what beauty is there in these figures of men with birds' heads, in these hideous distortions of human and animal forms? What nobility in a race whose supreme preoccupation, so far as we know, was the preservation of their bodies?

Loti had little that was fresh to say about Egypt, though, being Loti, he writes with charm. Here is the verdict of one of his own countrymen * on his book: "The reader accustomed to his earlier works is surprised at his persistent abuse of those who are attracted by the ruins of Egypt, and of those who are working to increase the productivity of the country. Progress, we agree, is not always favourable

* M. Serban.

to picturesqueness, but that is a trite commonplace which spoils, in our opinion, this particular work of Loti's. We miss here the mournful charm, the poignant tone, that fascinating suggestiveness, which lend so much beauty to his other books. The author's bad temper, in fact, seems to have dried up his emotional force. We should be tempted to regard this as a sign of decrepitude if he did not surpass himself in later productions. Instead, we may perceive here, the effects of an ill humour, fortunately short lived.''

The book was published in 1909. It may be that, having read it, somebody thought it worth while trying to convert the writer to a kinder and, I hope, truer, view of England. In July, 1909, we actually find Loti in London—to his own frankly-expressed astonishment. "England has, indeed, reserved for me surprises—the greatest being to find myself there! First, London—a city which I had sworn never to visit, but, of which I now flatter myself to be the discoverer." His last exclamation, and "the discoveries" that he announces, amount to an ingenuous confession that he had never sought to know anything about the country which he had been abusing for the greater part of his fifty-nine years. Yet the summer of that year, so unhappily typical of our climate, was hardly calculated to correct his ill opinion. But he was delighted with our parks, especially at the sight of the sheep grazing in them, at the leafiness of our squares, at the *rus in urbe* aspect of South Kensington and Knightsbridge. "Flowers everywhere!" he exclaims

"Every balcony, every window, is like a florist's window."

He found the architecture of our streets poor— apparently had no eye for the quiet dignity of Nash; but he had the good taste to perceive the sombre, majestic beauty of Westminster. Outside the West End he hardly seems to have ventured; he has nothing at all to say of the country which he traversed between Dover and Charing Cross.

Nor did he make the acquaintance of our people, but what he saw of them considerably modified his preconceptions. "There is so much good-nature among the wayfarers—and beyond doubt, *individually*, so much kindness. It is unfortunate that England should have entrusted the affairs of Egypt and the Transvaal to men of the predatory type, in whom are exaggerated the callousness and rapacity of the Anglo-Saxons taken *collectively*. But already the Transvaal has benefited by the personal good nature of the King, and the time may come when the yoke of the Egyptians may also be lifted. . . . "

He finds something graceful in the motion of our policemen's hands as they arrest the traffic. But his conversion is, of course, effected by contact with royalty.

At a ball at the French embassy, at which he arrived very late, one evening towards the end of July, he saw "a graceful woman of youthful outline, standing at the end of the room. She looked on, smiling. She wore a simple dress of some diaphanous black stuff, relieved at the hem with pale flame-coloured embroidery. When someone told me, 'That is the Queen,' I could hardly believe it—she looked so young."

Loti was presented while the dance went on. Queen Alexandra addressed him in the amiable tone "which sovereigns use towards the guests of their country.

"The next moment from another room, where he had been playing bridge, issued King Edward. 'Ah!' he exclaimed, smiling and holding out his hand as the ambassador presented me, 'so this is the Anglophobe!' 'Sire,' I replied, 'I am less so already.'"

Certainly someone must have told King Edward, for, in the absence of any inside information, I cannot conceive His late Majesty reading any one of our author's works. But the Queen had, for when, the next day, at his own request, Loti was received by her in private audience at Buckingham Palace, she began at once to talk about them. Remembering his attacks upon the English, he felt, he confesses, decidedly uncomfortable, and began to offer excuses. But Alexandra, with an air of confidence which touched him more than any reproaches, cut him short with the words: "That is all over now, is it not?" "Yes," replied the life-long Anglophobe, with an unpleasant recollection of certain articles then in the press, "that is all over now." Her Majesty took leave of him at the head of the stairs. The court had moved that day to Windsor, and Loti wandered a long time about the palace before he could find anyone to let him out.

If he had stayed longer in London, he might have found less flunkeyish reasons for revising his estimate of the English people. He was not too old to notice that the "Cookesses" are not representative of our womanhood—that as many (or more) pretty faces are to be seen in our streets as on the boulevard. Had he been younger, we might have had an idyll of Hyde Park. And he failed to notice, amazingly enough, the London cat—the pride and ornament of our homes! In our fondness for animals—our kindness for them (and I am not forgetful of our many and grievous inconsistencies in this respect) he might have found matter for genuine sympathy and admiration.

And yet . . . the doubt arises whether he ever would have liked us—or whether he would have made many friends among us. As a youth, he would have been most antipathetic to English lads. One cannot imagine him surviving an English public school, still less an English training ship. His sentimental point of view, his persistent idealisation of himself, would have exposed him over here to downright persecution. His mannerisms, his sensibility about his person, the vanity which prompted him as he grew older to use paint, like a Rumanian colonel, came in for bitter censure from his own countrymen— by the majority of Britons they would have been found simply intolerable. And if British sentimentality had been shocked by his frank identification of love with lust, no less would he have been disgusted by its essential disingenuousness, the obliqueness of our moral vision, particularly by certain stupid vulgar people's habit of speaking of Asiatics as "natives." On the whole, it is as well that he came late to this country and did not stay long.

As it was, his conversion by the smile of a charming queen was not lasting or sincere. He writes to his usual correspondent:

"It is quite true that the English have got round me, and that I shan't be able to go for them in future as I have done hitherto. But I am consoled by what I have already said about them. The woman who fascinated me most was the Queen. You must forgive me for having been over there. You need not fear that I am going to throw bouquets at them!"

So Mme. Adam, having devoted much of her long life to keeping alive enmity between France and Germany, did not want to encourage friendship with England, either. Of course, all this is no revelation to those who know the real France, and who realise, as Walpole did, the profound differences between the two nations; but it is a little pathetic, considered in the light of the burning enthusiasm for France and the French felt by millions of English people, and extravagantly expressed by a powerful section of our press during the war and the years that followed.

Still, Loti never forgot afterwards to temper his criticism of the "secular enemy" with some slight tribute to our "dignity and religious sense." It is satisfactory to know that Queen Alexandra's graciousness was not altogether wasted.

CHAPTER XXI

THE GATHERING DUSK

THE *Vautour* was Loti's last ship, as it was his last and only important command. From November 1905, till September, 1906, he was in charge of the naval depôt at his native place, to which he continued to be attached till January 14th, 1910, when, having reached the age limit, he was placed on the retired list. He had been promoted *capitaine de vaisseau* in August, 1906.

One is surprised, on examining his record, to find how much of a sailor this romantic novelist had been. M. Serban computes his service at forty-two years, three months, and thirteen days, of which not less than nineteen years, eleven months, and eight days had been spent at sea (two years, eight months and five days on active war service). And he found time to write twenty-eight books, not including the collection published this final year under the title *La Belle au Bois Dormant*.

The French navy was grateful for the lustre reflected on it by Captain Viaud. His career, remarked a service organ (*Revue Maritime*), would have been honourable enough, had it consisted only in that austere, exhausting, and obscure duty, discharged without the hope of glory, which is the sailor's lot in time of peace, and generally in time of war; but, in addition, by services rendered outside his profession, and by the number of valuable recruits whom he attracted to the navy, he deserved the last official comment upon him by Admiral Bugard, in 1906—"The recent promotion of Captain Viaud is the just reward of his service in the navy."

In partial confirmation of this professional testimony, M. Serban quotes a Parisian newspaper of the year 1888, which says that forty out of fifty schoolboys, when questioned as to their choice of a profession, chose the sea—a choice which is attributed to Loti's influence. That influence did not leave its mark on recent history; but it is obviously not his fault, whether the enthusiasm died down or whether the French Government diverted it into other channels. The comparison between Loti and de Vigny is familiar. It seems to me to exhibit as much dissimilarity as resemblance. The soldier consciously stressed the dignity of the profession of arms, even while illustrating its most sober and least picturesque side; Loti mostly glorifies the fisherman, and only incidentally touches on "the grandeurs and servitudes of the navy." We have the word of his commanders that he was an excellent officer. Notwithstanding, the literary critic might be tempted to see in de Vigny, the soldier at his desk, and in Loti, the man of letters aboard ship.

When, continues the naval review above quoted, Admiral Grasset visited the roads of La Pallice, in July, 1914, he invited Loti aboard his flagship, the *Jeanne d'Arc*, and held a reception in his honour. The master, in return, invited all the midshipmen of the vessel to his house. "The young officers, warmed with admiration and emotion, were inflamed as they listened to the accents of the immortal singer of the sea."

His retirement, though, of course, inevitable and long anticipated, was keenly felt by Loti.

Over a quarter of a century before, in that lugubrious sketch, *Un Vieux*, he had guessed at the feelings of a sailor upon his stripping himself of the uniform which had become a second skin. It had gone, that romantic character which fortified Loti against a sense of his own personal shortcomings. And, hardest to bear, here was an official, a positive intimation that he was an old man.

He turned, as is natural to some, to the scenes where he had been most the young man. In 1910, we find him again at Constantinople. But while he had left his youth behind him, Turkey hoped to renew hers. The old Sultan no longer brooded over the city, but sat, like Loti, recalling his young days, in a villa at Salonika. In his stead, ruled a commonplace, bourgeois-looking person, the puppet of the Young Turks. To Loti it seemed that the Stambul of Aziyade, the Stambul which he loved, had gone for ever. The process of Europeanization had begun. The friend of Islam could find little to approve in it. Most of all he condemned the ruthless

LOTI'S HOUSE AT ROCHEFORT : THE TURKISH SALON.

EXTERIOR OF LOTI'S HOUSE AT ROCHEFORT.

destruction of the dogs who had followed the victorious arms of Mohammed II to Byzantium, and had remained there ever since—"the dear dogs which one saw roving about everywhere, inoffensive and courteous, so grateful for the least caress. They mounted guard at night over their districts, cleaned the streets, and looked after the little children."*

The fate of the dogs, though bad enough, was not quite so horrible as it was described to him by an old Turk on the Asiatic side. Food was taken out to them at their place of banishment on an island in the Sea of Marmora, at the instance, I think, of an English society. But it is to the credit of the Turks themselves that they yielded only a reluctant obedience to the orders of the new Government in this matter, and even offered resistance in many cases, as recorded by Loti. He was not, therefore, under the sad necessity of changing his opinion of them as a people.

The Orient still held him under a spell. The streets of Stambul were better lighted, there seemed to be more animation; but (he writes), "no sooner was I seated in a humble little café facing the sea, among these dreamy folk, than upon me descended the ineffable peace of an Asiatic evening. It was not only my eyes which were soothed—no; the calm extended to my oriental soul which, after exile,

---

* In this important respect, resembling Barrie's delightful Nanna! I did not know the dogs of Constantinople were as useful as all this, but they certainly deserved everybody's sympathy. I remember seeing them sitting in a row along the quay of Galata, waiting open-mouthed for the biscuits they expected passengers to throw them. One evening one of them slipped along the gangplank unobserved and curled himself up snugly in my bunk. His expression when I found him I can only describe as wheedling. Needless to say, I left him undisturbed till I wanted to go to bed myself.—E.B. d'A.

found itself at home again. And the terrifying flight of time seemed to have slowed up, almost to have stopped, among these things which were just the same a hundred years ago, amidst these calm people who live and pray as their ancestors did, who can only guess at their own age, and mark the hour only by the muezzin's call."

He dwelt in an old Turkish house built on piles on the Asiatic shore of the Bosporus, at Candilli, and visited old friends. The Turkish woman had not lost her charm for him, he had to admit, even when she dined with him at friends' tables, in quite the European manner, and did not hesitate to lift her veil—though the blinds were drawn that old-fashioned people might not be scandalised. He found these new *Turques* quite charming—he reserved his opinion on the New *Turc*. No, Constantinople had not changed—yet.

He rambled about the old familiar byways, and haunted the spots sanctified by the loves six years and thirty-four years past. He tells us, as I have said, that he inquired after the heroine of the latter romance. But strive after the fatalism of Islam though he might, he was oppressed by a sense of finality. "Alas! Time stays, we go!" complained a poet. The old sailor looked across the Bosporus and remembered his last ship. "I shall not know that floating home again," he sighs, "where I ruled as king, though not as a tyrant. Gone, disintegrated, destroyed beyond hope of restoration! The ship broken up and sold piecemeal in France—my officers, my crew, scattered about the four quarters of the globe, never to be reunited. To think of it makes my heart ache a little."

What can the man of sixty expect when he goes on such a pilgrimage? His only interest can lie in the next generation. Loti's tired heart leaped at the sight of his son, now a youth of twenty-one, who came to see the city his father loved so well. "It is first-rate, this place!" (*C'est rudement chic ici !*) was the young man's comment, looking around. With a confidence rare between father and son—rarer, perhaps, among the English than the French—Loti showed Samuel Viaud the grave of Aziyade.

He had lost much to the merciless years, but they had brought him a good friend in his son. This he realised anew when he fell ill of a fever. Sitting in the garden of the French consulate during convalescence he watched the summer decline, and with it, as it seemed to him, his life.

He went back to France, and thought what he should do next. It was time to write the account of his journey to Angkor. But chance only, he tells us, led him upstairs to the "museum."

" . . . a room which I never think of looking into, but which I allow to remain as a sort of memory's garden. The little things which, in days gone by, used to make me think of places far away, have dried up and are crumbling in their cases. . . . I detect an odour of camphor, of stuffed birds, somewhat of death; it is unspeakably sad in here. But it is even more depressing when I have admitted the rays of the evening autumn sun.

"Yet it was certainly decisive, the influence which this museum exercised upon my life. It is the same with all men, all of them the puppets of their first impressions. Little things, persistently dwelt upon in childhood, suffice to sway, one way or another, the course of their life.

"Ah! here is that colonial magazine which first spoke to me of Angkor. How crude on the yellowing paper appear the illustrations in comparison with those we are accustomed to nowadays! Yes, they are half a century old, alas! Yet they are faithful enough; there is the tiara of tall towers which I have actually seen in the substance. . . . And the pictures naturally recall the impressions which they first excited in me; even those emphatic phrases borrowed from the Ecclesiast which echoed in my childish brain, ' I have tried everything, experienced everything. . . . In the depths of the forests of Siam, I have seen the star of eve rising above the ruins of the mysterious Angkor. . . .'

"Eh? But to-day . . . but this, this, now, is my return to the old home which I forsaw so clearly! —the final return with a tired heart and whitening hair. It is no illusion. It is to-day, and the cycle of my life is closed."

CHAPTER XXII

APOTHEOSIS

BUT thirteen years remained to him, and these were full of honour.

In 1911, Italy, without the shadow of an excuse, seized Tripoli, which, inhabited by a purely Muslim population, had formed part of the Ottoman Empire for centuries. Too old to draw the sword in defence of Islam, Loti reached for his pen and denounced this infamous act of piracy. A long article by him was admitted to the *Figaro* (January 3rd, 1911). "The Muslims," he remarks, "in the eyes of Christendom appear to be game which may be hunted at any season." As to atrocities—he has no doubt that the Italians are not guiltless.

An Italian had the audacity to write inquiring whether he did not admire this evidence of Latin enterprise. Loti replied in scathing terms. To his mortification, his "second mother", who could find no palliation for the misdeeds of Britain and Germany, sided with the Italians. The correspondence between these aging people became, for a while, acrimonious. "I must indeed love you, *madame chérie*," he writes on January 21st, 1912, "to kiss your hands after your professions of cannibalism!" But "after all, theirs is an affection which has withstood many assaults."

This year (1912) he produced only his *Pélerin d'Angkor*—his premature Nunc dimittis. His preoccupation with political events, or rather with the political interests of his adopted country, became more intense upon the outbreak of the much more serious war between Turkey and the confederated Balkan states. With dismay he watched the progress of the campaign—the retreat of the Ottomans under pressure from front, flank, and rear, the fall of Salonica and Adrianople, the battles in Thrace, the hemming-in of Turkey behind the rampart of Chatalja. In this rude hour, the Turks were well served by Loti. Reckless of the enmity he excited in powerful quarters, reckless of the risk to which he was subjecting his popularity, he carried on a strenuous propaganda in the French press. Now, no war has been carried on since the beginning of this century without both sides accusing each other of committing atrocities. Whether the press considers it best serves its country by inventing these— whether they are and always have been inseparable from war, and that we have only just awakened to them—or whether they are peculiar to our own generation, it is unwise to say. There is strong impartial testimony that this particular war was conducted with fiendish cruelty—on both sides, most people will say, but Loti maintained that the Christians were the more serious, almost the only offenders. He was supplied with plenty of evidence, raw and smoking, from Constantinople. The Bulgarians he charged with unnameable atrocities, which is strange, because an American committee of inquiry held them less guilty than their allies, and they were found by the British, four and five years after, to be fairly clean fighters.

Some sort of protests were made by the French enemies of the Turks. Loti stated that atrocities by the confederates had actually been witnessed by an officer of the battleship *Bruix* at Salonica. This was contradicted by the captain of the *Bruix* in a letter to Prince Nicholas of Greece. This brought Farrère to the relief of his old chief with assertions upon his honour as a French officer, and other chivalrous flourishes. But the Bulgarians were equally sensitive. A young lieutenant at Sofia addressed a formal challenge to Loti in the name of the Bulgarian army, naming two seconds in France who were to call on him. One would not have been surprised if our author had accepted; to have crossed swords with the foe of Turkey in the name of Aziyade would have been a fine finish-up for an eminently picturesque career. After all, within his memory, two middle-aged statesmen, Boulanger and Floquet, had fought in the Bois de Boulogne. Instead, Loti replied through the columns of the *Figaro* and *Gil Blas*. It was a challenge, he said, which he would have been the first to take up when he was young; at his age (he was sixty-two), it was not to be thought of; besides the lieutenant's letter was couched in terms that did not merit consideration; he had consigned it to the waste-paper basket and his seconds, if they called, would be shown the door. There was always the method of assassination, he suggested, with which the Balkan Christians should be familiar. The Bulgar's challenge was disavowed by Tsar Ferdinand; and Loti went on abusing the Bulgarians till the end of the war, and ever afterwards.

The confederates, we know, turned their arms against each other. In the summer of 1913, while Turkey was awaiting the issue of the peace negotiations, Loti paid his farewell visit to Constantinople. Had he restored to them all their lost provinces, the Ottomans could not have shown themselves more grateful. No man of letters in any age or any country has received so generous and splendid a recognition from any people.

He was received like a king, says one biographer—rather, I should say, like a conquering hero. The streets were lined with troops. Banners waved in the air. Rich carpets were spread for him to walk on, beneath festoons and garlands. Crowds frantically shouted their greetings. Every section of the population was represented. Even the *hammals* or porters came in procession to do him honour. From the Top Hane quay, where he remembered to have landed as a midshipman nearly forty years before, he was carried off in the imperial launch, amid the frenzied plaudits of the public. The Sultan took his own watch and chain from his pocket and attached it to Loti's waistcoat. Banquets, receptions, demonstrations followed. Loti took his place in a magnificent state barge, with Heaven-knows-how-many rowers, and made a triumphal progress along the shores of the Bosporus, every village illuminating and decorating in honour of the Friend of Islam. "For the moment, I am an oriental prince!" he exclaims. In this hour of his apotheosis, he must have remembered his dreams in the attic at Rochefort. Even his boyish imagination had not pictured this! and he had thought his life finished, that there was nothing more to come. . . .

At Adrianople, recently re-conquered from the Bulgars, the same reception awaited him.

He returned to Stambul, and was admitted to the innermost recesses of mosque, vizierate, and palace. All doors flew open before him. He was received at the historic Seraglio, and saw the lamps which marked the spots where bygone sultans and viziers had been murdered. It had been proposed to offer him quarters here, a jolly old eunuch informed him, but it was feared he would find them too cold and gloomy. Loti, in fact, would have been delighted to stay in lodgings so historical, in the very palace of the house of Osman.

It gave him pleasure to take a house, instead, in the neighbourhood of the mosque of Sultan Selim, to which, in the old days, he hardly dared to penetrate. Now he prayed publicly in the mosque itself, and was asked by the dervishes and imams why he did not formally become a Muslim. He does not say why—but behind and below his passion for the East there was always his loyalty to those Huguenot ancestors of his lying out on the isle in the Atlantic.

At this house, he received a visit from his old friend Zennur. She came, accompanied by two of her sisters, and a negress. In Paris she had looked so much like a Parisienne; it was strange, now, to see her more Turkish in her attire than in the days of *The Désenchantées*. Apparently, the secret confided to her by Marc Hélys, was still well kept. Loti entertained his visitors, Turkish fashion, with little cups of coffee. Two carriages were in waiting below. "I assisted the ladies and their attendant into one," says Loti, "and got into the other, all this without troubling about the policemen who were looking on, or the children of the quarter who had collected round. Times have changed since Abd-ul-Hamid spread terror and oppression around him."

Loti, we see, had reconsidered his estimate of the Young Turks. But, for a brief interval, he came near to renouncing not only them but the whole well-beloved Islam. Going on pilgrimage to the tomb of his "dear dead," he could not find it! His distress and indignation, he confesses thereat, were unbounded. "An immense disgust at once possessed me for this Turkey which I had so much loved. The secret of my love for the East lay in those two gravestones and the ashes that were beneath. Now this was profaned, I could only curse this country, to which nothing any longer attached me, where I had no longer any interests. I determined to leave by the next steamer, never to return."

It must be admitted that Loti, in his declining years, was becoming a trifle peevish and crotchety.

Further inquiry was made by his anxious Turkish friends, and it turned out that he had gone to the wrong cemetery! Almost joyously, he was driven in a carriage to the right place, and shown the real tomb, which the Turks had taken care to paint and gild anew, glittering in the moonlight. Over the grave of Aziyade, Loti renewed his friendship with Islam.

In his account of this last visit to the city of his love he relates a tender little anecdote of a starving kitten which he cared for, and which died, notwithstanding, on the knees of his son, Samuel. "Its little mind, its little consciousness, its little tenderness, who knows where they have gone!" he murmurs. But why did such episodes occur to Loti only in foreign countries? Cats are to be met with dying of starvation on the pavements of Paris and in the shadow of her churches. Let us hope he had befriended French cats as well as Turkish.

And on September 17th, amid fresh demonstrations of gratitude and friendship, he sailed for home. "Perhaps I shall return," he said hopefully. This time he was mistaken.

CHAPTER XXIII

THE UNSUCCESSFUL PLAYWRIGHT

In the autumn of 1912, between his two last visits to the Levant, Loti crossed the Atlantic for the first time since his boyhood. America, it need not be said, did not attract him. He went to New York to superintend the rehearsals of his drama, *The Daughter of Heaven*.

This seems as good a place as any other to deal with our author's efforts as a playwright. They dated as far back as 1893. Even before that, it appears that some unauthorized person staged a farcical version of *Frère Yves* at some fifth-rate Parisian theatre. Loti first heard of it through a notice in a newspaper by Jean Lorrain, who pronounced it side-splitting. "Can you tell me where I can see it?" very reasonably inquired the original author, "as I should like to split my sides, too." But by that time, the piratical burlesque had disappeared from the boards.

Two sketches—*L'Oeuvre de Pen Brom, dated* 1891, and *La Grotte d'Isturitz,* 1893—are mentioned as theatrical works by him, but seem not to have been produced. But on February 18th, 1893, a dramatised version of *Pêcheur d'Islande,* written by Loti in collaboration with Louis Tiercelin, in four acts, was produced at the Grand Theatre, Paris. From the first, the critics seem to have let Loti down lightly; but "Uncle Sarcey," writing in the *Temps*, admits that the play has not found favour with the public. "To-day (Feb. 27th) the house is empty." But it seems to have struggled on till March 4th, as an occasional item in the bill.

Madame Chrysanthème, a lyrical comedy in four acts, adapted from Pierre Loti, by G. Hartmann and A. Alexandre, with music by André Messager, had been produced on January 31st, at the Theatre Lyrique, the same year, but had a very short run. A much more ambitious attempt was Loti's own drama, *Judith Renaudin*, founded on the experiences of one of his Huguenot ancestors during the persecution under Louis XIV. This piece is included in the author's complete works, and was put on at the Thèatre Antoine on November 2nd, 1898. The critic, Robert de Flers, politely dismisses it thus: "*Judith Renaudin* will not add to Loti's glory, but we are glad of this opportunity to renew our respectful admiration for the author!"

Earlier in the year (1898), *L'Ile du Rêve*, a musical version of *Rarahu*, by Loti, Hartmann and Alexandre with music by Reynaldo Hahn, had been staged at the Opera Comique. Damned by faint praise, it ran for four weeks from March 23rd. It should have been obvious from the first that no play was to be made out of the book. But theatrical producers in every country have a rare instinct for the undramatic.

This last failure seems to have discouraged Loti for a considerable time. His friend Juliette, however, made him an honorary director of her own theatre, afterwards destroyed by fire, and, in her correspondence with him, she inserts letters from him to Claretie and others referring to possible plays from his pen. In middle life, he turned his attention to tragedy, and made himself responsible, in collaboration with Emile Védel, for a translation of *King Lear*. He offered this to Claretie, observing that it was by one Shakspere and had a lot of Shakspere in it. It found a producer in Antoine, who took the title rôle, on December 6th, 1904; but it had only a very short run.

Ramuntcho, as one might expect, was more of a success on the stage. In five acts, with music by Gabriel Pierné, it was staged at the Odéon by André Antoine, on Febuary 29th, 1908, and did not disappear from the bill till March 24th. It had a pretty good press. Jean Richepin in *Comoedia* recommends it to the public that appreciates poetry, dreams and beauty. Faguet, in the *Débats*, describes it as a picturesque, rather than dramatic, poem, but advises everyone to go and see it. Generally speaking, it was pronounced to be a fine spectacle, but no play. Brisson in the *Temps* says it was a pity that Loti did not seek the collaboration of *un homme du métier*.

Wandering about the forlorn palaces of Peking, Loti first conceived the idea of a work dealing with the imperial race of China. It is to be regretted that he did not express that idea in a novel. Instead, in collaboration with a brilliant actress, Judith Gautier, the daughter of Théophile, he turned it into a drama. Claude Farrère tells us that he was shown the script while aboard the *Vautour*, and asked by Loti for his opinion. The young officer was so struck with its sublimity that he returned it without presuming on a criticism—a gesture which the author mistook for condemnation.

Certain people afterwards must have regretted he was not so far discouraged as to put it in the fire. I can find no evidence of the play having been produced in Paris; but it was to attend the production at the Century Theatre of an English translation by George Egerton,* under the title of *The Daughter of Heaven*, that Loti, at the age of sixty-two, undertook the journey to New York. In his account of his visit, he gives us to understand that his play met with an enthusiastic reception. It is pronounced, however, by one American authority to have been "the most colossal failure of the year. The piece was not at all dramatic, and was lacking in the English version even in literary merit. It was lavishly produced, but the sumptuous scenery served more as an encumbrance to the story than an illustration." The *American Yearbook* refers to it in these terms: "An unfortunate spectacular fiasco was Geo. C. Tyler's sumptuous production of the *Daughter of Heaven* by Pierre Loti and Judith Gautier. There was too much China, too many long speeches about the unity of the yellow races, and too little real passion or play."

* The pen-name of Mrs. Bright.

Yet it was produced at the right moment, when the downfall of the Manchus and the proclamation of a republic had quickened the interest of the western world in things Chinese. Chinese students, many of them the sons of rich merchants, so Loti tells us, were proud to walk on as supers. A curate, who had just given up the Church for the stage, took the part of a mandarin.* During the rehearsals, American girls sat in the wings and interviewed the author. He was amazed at their self-possession, the extent of their travels, and their continuous munching of sandwiches and chocolates. He was also struck by the "correctness" of the little theatre girls who conducted themselves like girls of good society. At the conclusion of the performance he was called before the curtain with Viola Allen, who took the leading part.

He was unconscious, apparently, of his failure—or adroitly conceals it from his French readers. And he certainly shows no bitterness against a city which must have been intensely antipathetic to him. He did not like it ; he describes it as a pandemonium. Even when he drove out into the country he was pained at the sight of so many plants unfamiliar to him. But he admired Riverside Drive, and was delighted to see squirrels running wild and unmolested in Central Park. One wishes he had visited our St. Johns Wood. The city achieves, he says, a certain tragic beauty by the very excess of its horror. He was amused by the queries to which he had to reply before landing : "Are you a polygamist?"

* *New York Herald.*

"Are you not a congenital idiot?" etc., and gives a highly diverting account of being interviewed by an army of reporters. He answered through an interpreter, but two women arrived who were able to speak French also, and these added to his bewilderment by cross-examining him while the major examination was proceeding. Among the questions on which he was asked to give his views he mentions the suffragettes, the castration of criminals, proportional representation, and the methods of attack of the rhinoceros.

By the *New York Herald* man he was treated, at any rate, better than a good many distinguished foreigners. His arrival is described in that journal under date September 22nd, 1912. " 'Well, it looks as if they had something on Mr. Vernier,'" commented a passenger who had just stepped off the liner Savoie on to the pier, " 'I was suspicious of him all the way out. I am always suspicious of anyone who can't speak English.'" "Mr. Vernier" was the alias under which Loti had travelled. His fellow-traveller's comment was provoked by the sight of him surrounded by the reporters and custom-house officers at the same time. Followed by twenty-two reporters he took refuge in the Marie Antoinette Hotel. "His interviewers were having a hard time with him till the only reporter in New York who wore a silk hat appeared."

The information was then extracted from Loti's companion and interpreter, M. François de Tessan, that the great author made from $35,000 to $40,000 a year arising out of his books. And "as no newspaper article will be written within the next few weeks without mention of his feet, be it said that they really are small."

A week later, we learn from the same journal that the eminent writer was a trifle more communicative. But he is still keeping close to his room at the Marie Antoinette. He has seen nobody except Geo. C. Tyler, the hotel clerk, and the reporters, but hopes to soon. "Already the famous novelist, dramatist, and academician has written O.K. over the picture of that part of New York which he has seen. This part includes the advertising signs along Broadway and the fifty young women who are rehearsing at the Century Theatre.

"Nobody has reserved the right to admire New York girls. Everybody does it and all are proud of it. So it was only to be expected that Mr. Loti would fall immediately into the habit. He also appreciates the New York idea in admiration, which is not to specialize on any one girl, or very many girls anyhow.

"'The young women,' he said, 'are very much more beautiful, graceful, and intelligent than I supposed. They seem to be witty, but I cannot understand what they are saying.'" Asked whether he thought Broadway would be improved by the removal of all the electric signs, Loti is reported to have said no. Certain of the signs amused and interested him enormously, and he had stood looking at them some time.

"He says nothing about his age—in fact, he seems anxious to conceal it," goes on the 'cute reporter, "but he let slip the fact that he spent twenty-four hours here in New York about forty years ago. The only thing he doesn't like in New York is three reporters." He complained of certain papers' treatment of him. "I do not try to make fun of America and Americans—and I do not think they should make fun of me."

The same paper announces that the distinguished Frenchman was going to Washington to lunch with President Taft and the French ambassador. Loti himself tells us nothing of that.

He had lunch with the dons of Columbia University beside which institution the French universities seemed mere provincial academies, and received an address from the Alliance française. But confessing himself to be just an old Oriental, he was extremely relieved when he found himself once more on his familiar element, with the sky-scrapers of New York going down behind the narrows and the sandy low-lying shore.

He probably never read the "interview" with him published next day in the *New York Herald*. It represents him as talking American with the idiomatic fluency of a Bowery tough. As a contribution to American imaginative literature, it ranks high indeed.

CHAPTER XXIV

LOTI LEAVES US

AT sixty-four years of age, Loti might well look forward to a few more years of lettered ease. He passed most of his time at Hendaye, of which town he had long become the tutelary genius, defending it tenaciously against the designs of the builder and speculator. The attempt to turn the place into a fashionable seaside resort roused his ire, and brought him into collision with local interests. Meanwhile, he strove to keep alive the Basque customs and traditions, and encouraged the national game of pelota—though, he mourned, the young men seemed to prefer the coarse and vulgar football. A long while before (1899) he had bought back the ancient house on the isle of Oléron which had been the home of his ancestors. Here again he fell foul of the Communal authorities, who stupidly prohibited the pretty local custom of planting flowers outside the houses along the inner edge of the pavement.

In the midst of these petty disputes, not uncommon with elderly gentlemen of artistic and conservative views, he was roused by the first thunderclaps of the world war.

PIERRE LOTI'S HOUSE AT ROCHEFORT : THE MOSQUE.

THE HOUSE OF JUDITH RENAUDIN, AT ST. PIERRE D'OLÉRON, IN THE GARDEN
OF WHICH PIERRE LOTI IS BURIED.

As I have said, it was his destiny to be too late for actual fighting. Still, he thought there was a chance . . . Samuel went off to join his battery. The old sailor wondered whether, after all, he might not die in action—"the only death which is not sad and terrifying." He presented himself before the admiral at Rochefort and was given a job—in the arsenal. This did not satisfy him. He appealed to the Minister of Marine.

"In a country where everyone is doing his duty so admirably, I do not wish to set a bad example by doing nothing. My double capacity makes my position a little exceptional. Pardon me, then, if I solicit an exceptional favour. I will accept with joy and pride any post in presence of the enemy, even one very much inferior to what my rank entitles me.

"At the worst, could I not be sent in some supernumerary capacity aboard some ship likely to be in action? I should find a way of making myself useful, I do assure you. Or, if even that is contrary to the regulations, I might, at least, be allowed to help where best I could, in an ambulance, for instance, while waiting for employment in the fleet. It is certainly hard that because I happen to be a captain on the reserve list I should be condemned to inaction while all France is in arms."

The ministry, as was the universal practice of ministries at the beginning of the war, rejected such appeals for employment with disdain. But Loti commanded influence which overrode the decrees of the bureaucrats of the Rue Royale. On February

1st, 1915, Captain Viaud was mobilised, and attached to the headquarter staff of General Galliéni, the governor of Paris.

Loti's fighting days had long gone by. What active service he had seen was on sea, not on land. It cannot be supposed that he was of much real use to the army. Very possibly, in his anxiety to help, he often got in the way. But it is not at all creditable to a leading French literary review that a man, named Louis Cario, should have been allowed, in its pages to expose an old officer and distinguished man of letters to ridicule—and that while the mould on his grave was still fresh. Loti, as Claude Farrère puts it, hated the indecencies of age; he did not like to look ugly: and his efforts at improving his appearance undoubtedly made him a butt for cheap humour. Cario seems to have found much that was laughable in Loti's dress and appearance; we find a good deal that is noble in his endeavours to help his country in her hour of need.

His footsteps may be traced all along that far-flung western front. Near Ypres he visited the King of the Belgians at his very modest headquarters; and though he had met many kings, never, he says, was he more deeply conscious of the royal dignity than on the threshold of that humble little house. He saw Reims and Soissons in the autumn of '15; the next year he was in Alsace, whence he writes to Juliette Adam, asking her to tell him how the people came to speak German when they were really French—he wanted to write a tract to the Alsatians, and never could remember historical data! He took a glance at the Somme, says little about the English, and delivered an address at the Comédie Française.

In the summer of 1916, he was despatched on a mission of some importance to the Italian front. He met King Victor Emmanuel, of course, and also Eleonora Duse. At Venice he stayed, as before, at Danieli's, and while keeping a look-out for Austrian aircraft, indulged his memories of Carmen Sylva. These missions and duties do not seem very onerous, but he was no longer in the prime of life and presently broke down. He went home on sick leave. "I have been very ill," he writes in a letter published by M. Serban. "For a fortnight past I have seen death sitting at my bedside. Now I am on my feet again, wonderful to relate, and hope soon to get back to the front. Better, perhaps, to have died than to witness the agony of France since the hideous desertion of those horrible Russians. I am anxious, too, about my little Samuel, who is still at the post of danger."

Samuel Viaud won his *croix de guerre,* and a commission about the middle of 1918. Loti had been definitely invalided out in May. On November 8th, hearing prematurely of the armistice, he wrote to Juliette, "Let us embrace and dance the Carmagnole! I find myself weeping; and you? Never before have I known the sensation of weeping for joy."

As a lad, and again as an old man, he had done what he could to help France against her deadliest foe. In both cases the part assigned to him had been insignificant. It was certainly honourable.

There may be some, hearafter, to wish that at this stage his activities had been purely military. For all the while he was fighting, as he hoped, with his pen. His wartime experiences, emotions, and opinions are embodied in two books entitled, *L'Hyéne Enragée* and *L'Horreur Allemande*. They are animated by that violent extravagant patriotism, that hysterical hatred, that utter indifference to truth, which already make sane men fidget uneasily. Did we really believe the nonsense we talked and wrote, ten years ago? Loti, I am afraid, was capable of believing in the Angels of Mons, The Crucified Canadian, and the German corpse-factory. The marvel is that he was not officially employed in some propaganda department of the Allied armies. But I am sorry he went about preaching the gospel of hate even to children and adjuring them never to forgive or forget.

But how much had he forgotten and forgiven himself? The war made strange bedfellows. When he lauded the gallant Italians, he had presumably sponged out of his memory their treacherous attack on Tripoli which he had so loudly denounced. He found himself apologising to the Serbs. While on the subject of atrocities, did he not recall certain doings of the French in Annam, chronicled by him in the *Figaro* ?

He had forgotten little. His sympathies emerged from the international melée, intact. As far back as August, 1914, he had replied to Juliette Adam's condemnation of the Turks, then on the point of joining the Central Powers. "What do the Turks

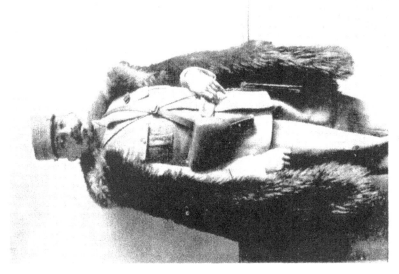

LOTI IN COLONEL'S UNIFORM (1915-18).

LOTI IN HIS GARDEN WITH HIS CATS.

owe to us? For thirty years past we have shown nothing but ingratitude and ignorance towards a people who have always extended the most cordial hospitality towards our citizens, our educational establishments, our language, while their neighbours, the Orthodox, have never ceased to injure us by trickery and infamy.

"It's the Turk who has the right to cry shame on France. It is we who allowed the English to steal Egypt. It's we who egged on the Italians in Tripoli. . . . In the matter of the German cruisers, the Turks have acted tactlessly and illegally, but not vilely."

And before the armistice with them was actually signed, Loti was speaking on behalf of his beloved Muslims—representing them as the weak but amiable victims of German guile. He had courage, in those hectic days of 1918, to champion a beaten foe! He was reminded by the *New York Herald* that he was conducting an agitation on behalf of a power which was still officially at war with France, and was described on the title page of a book issued in 1919 as "Pierre Loti, the friend of the massacrers." But he stuck to his Turks through thick-and-thin, with the blind partnership which had inspired his denunciations of the English and the Germans. For that matter, who cared twopence for truth or justice in those days of the Versailles conference? Loti, at least, made himself ridiculous by his advocacy of the defeated while the others were trampling the life out of their fallen foes and spouting lies while they did it.

In August, 1920, he had the happiness of assisting at the marriage of his son with the daughter of Vice-Admiral Charlier, commanding the Mediterranean fleet. He returned to the old home at Rochefort, very weak and ailing. "Nothing exhausts and takes it out of me so much as indignation," he complains; and the treatment of the beloved nation by Clemenceau cut him to the quick. He raved against the Greeks—cried out that the Turks had been thrown to them to satisfy the infernal voracity of the monstrous English, almost outdid Fleet Street in his abuse of King Constantine and Queen Sophia. (He had been pleased to lunch with this king's father in December 1903). In this year he published his *Mort de Notre Chère France en Orient*—a vigorous but unconvincing apology for the Turks—and in the following year, *Suprêmes Visions d'Orient* (in collaboration with his son). In '19 he had brought out *Prime Jeunesse*—the record of his boyhood, and was engaged in the last months of his life upon its sequel, *Un Jeune Officer Pauvre*. But a new, unsentimental generation had grown up, to which his works made less appeal. His last book went only into thirty-one impressions, as against the one hundred and five of the Egyptian book, and the four hundred and nineteen of *Désenchantées*.

What pictures must have shaped themselves in the old man's mind as he sat smoking his narghile before the imagined portrait of Aziyade in his wonderful Turkish chamber! His house, which had absorbed its neighbours, has been described as an Aladdin's palace. It was Loti's object to recreate within its walls foreign environments which had most charmed him. With the remnants of a mosque demolished at Damascus, he constructed a far more beautiful mosque, here in his own home. There you may see the turbeh or headstone of the best-beloved, before which a light was kept burning. I have spoken already of the Gothic hall; and there is another in renaissance style. In striking contrast to both is a vast Chinese hall in red and gold, adjoining a pagoda, both filled with the spoils of Peking. And everywhere, objects rare and beautiful, arms presented by the Sultan of Oman or other exotic prince, gifts from the Commander of the Faithful. . . .

More interesting, to my mind, was the odd little grotto built by big brother Gustave for a little boy's amusement, the mother's bedroom, and the typical provincial salon in red velvet, where Loti's bourgeois forbears, entering at any moment, would have found themselves at home. In the garden you may see the spot where lie buried a long succession of "Moumoutes" (all the cats of the Loti household bore that name, down to the last, found in, and brought back from, the trenches).

His love for Aziyade was genuine enough now. All the other women had faded out of mind; to the old man she had come to represent woman, youth, all that was sweet and glorious in life, all that had passed irrecoverably.

His old shipmate and literary colleague, Claude Farrère, has given us a touching account of the visit paid in December, 1921, to apprize him that he had

been awarded the Grand Cross of the Legion of
Honour, upon a petition signed by Pierre Louys,
Victor Margueritte, Pierre Mille, and other men of
letters. He found the old man very feeble, almost
speechless. The sailors groaned in concert over the
reduction of the French navy, and the mess the
politicians had made of Europe. Farrère was there
when a mission from Turkey—from the new Turkey
of Angora—arrived, composed of a secretary and a
fascinating woman; Madame Ferid Bey, the wife of
the ambassador. Loti scanned her handsome
features for some likeness to the dead. Much
moved, she spoke in Turkish at his request. At one
time, for a long period, so one of the sailor servants
whispered to Farrère, the commandant had spoken
with difficulty, and Turkish seemed to come more
easily to him than French.

One likes to know that Turkey was loving and
grateful to the last. The constitution of that
country had changed beyond recognition since Loti
had caught sight of those green eyes through the
lattices at Salonica; but, empire or republic, orthodox
or liberal, in good fortune and in adversity, the sons
of Osman stood by the man who had stood by them.
Their loyalty goes far to convert us to Loti's own
estimation of them.*

If not for theirs, we may be glad for Loti's sake
of the turn which events were soon to take. The
Greeks were routed—Smyrna, all Asia Minor, saved
for Islam; alone among the lately defeated nations,

---

* My friend, Mr. W. R. H. Trowbridge, who has returned from Constantinople
as I am passing these proofs, tells me that Loti continues to be spoken of with
love and respect by the Turks of all classes.

Turkey had raised her head, and with hand on the hilt of her sword, dealt on an equal footing with the diplomatists of Europe at the council board. Did Loti know of this? One hopes he did. But it was not given him to know of Turkey's final crowning success at Lausanne. At the beginning of June, 1923, profiting by a slight apparent improvement in his health, he insisted on being taken to Hendaye. There, some fortune-teller had warned him, death awaited him. "I am happy, quite happy," he murmured, pressing the hands of his friends on his arrival. "The next day, his medical man pronounced him to be better, and it was hoped that he might recover a certain amount of strength in a country and among friends so dear to him. Vain hope! In the evening he was invaded by an ominous torpor, and the struggle with the black phantom began at once. It was long, because of his astonishing vitality. But there was nothing of the supreme terror, of which he had so often spoken. Little by little, we saw his life ebb, the light gradually fade from his face. Sunday, towards four o'clock (June 10th, 1923), he breathed his last . . . in the presence of his own people, of some old friends, and of his faithful sailor servants who had cared for him with unfailing and touching devotion."*

His second mother was with him at the end. "He preserved," she tells us, "all his intelligence, his sensibility, his filial tenderness, so much of which he had lavished on me. He told me, in reply to my question, that he had nothing more to ask of life

* Emile Vedel L'Illustration, June 23rd, 1923.

now he saw his son happy and had held his grandson in his arms. And in leaving one mother, he *believed* that he was about to meet the other."

Did he, in fact, find faith at the last moment? Was the death which he had so much dreaded rendered less terrible by the hope of a further life? His friend, Louis Barthou, says, no. "Pierre Loti, born a Protestant, remained so out of respect for family tradition and affection for his ancestors. But he had not the faith. He had sought it without attaining it."

It was among those ancestors that he had planned to rest. That he had little enough in common with them he well knew. "You have sprung from their house," Alphonse Daudet had once told him, "like a demon from out a trap-door. All those generations, stifled by their regularity of life, are now frantically gasping for breath through you.* You are paying the penalty, Loti, and it's not your fault." Three years before his death he had chosen his grave—"at the end of the garden of our ancestral home, at the foot of the myrtle, on the right hand side going towards the shrubbery." Already he had had his gravestone prepared—it was engraved simply with the name Pierre Loti.

And to this last, deep, peaceful bed, on the island in the heaving grey Atlantic, he was borne on June 16th. Brought back to the house in which he was born, his frail body had lain all night in the Gothic hall, guarded by two of the bluejackets he had loved so well. Covered by the tricolour flag, the coffin

* But Loti was also the son of his father, a fact which both he and his friends always overlooked.

was conveyed on a gun-carriage to the riverside escorted by sailors and marines, where it was carried aboard the despatch-boat, *Chamois*. Along the banks of the Charente the people saluted and threw flowers at the passing ship. Across a rough sea steamed the *Chamois*, escorted now by four torpedo boats. At St. Pierre d'Olèron, in the little "temple" where the Renaudins and Texiers had worshipped, the pastor pronounced a short prayer. And in the dusk—such a dusk, perhaps, as that in which he had seen his life spread out before him— when the crowds and the soldiers had departed, Pierre Loti was laid in the earth by his son and a few faithful sailors.

"I desire," he had written in his will," that the public shall not be allowed to visit my grave. Twice a year it may be visited by ten persons, the list of whom shall be given by my son or his heirs to the successive tenants of our old home, who shall be the guardians of my sepulchre."

"Seven hundred leagues away," says Claude Farrère, "on a slope studded with wild cypresses, I know a little Turkish tomb which four pious men— three Musulmans and one Christian—are charged to maintain and preserve, so long as they, and after them their sons, shall live. A very small tomb— two stones facing each other, of white marble—a mysterious epitaph deeply cut—and that is all. It is forty-three years since that tomb was closed upon the body of a Circassian girl. . . .

"The man went on living; but devoured by torturing melancholy. Time and again he returned to that childish tomb. Flowers grew meanwhile upon it. Last December, some cornflowers, born thus of the body of Aziyade, were sent from Stambul to Rochefort. And Loti touched them with his hands."

The most unfortunate of men, Farrère elsewhere calls him. Why, his career was the most enviable a mortal can conceive! He lived to see all his ambitions realised and transcended. He tasted the ecstacies of love, he turned the pages of the great picture-book and found them enthralling. What made him unhappy? Was it remorse for the abandonment of Aziyade?—the fear of extinction? Only his intimates, and perhaps not they, can answer positively. I half suspect it was that persistent consciousness of insufficiency. One recalls him as he stood, abashed, wistful, suppliant, before the veiled women on the waterside at Therapia—his lament that he was not handsome. Never did he become the hero he had hoped to be. Measured by his own standards, he found himself wanting, frustrate, ridiculous. They may not have been exalted standards, but they were his own. He had chosen to be a sailor, and as a sailor he cut a respectable, but never a heroic figure. Who knows whether he would not have exchanged his academic palm for the laurel? Yearning for one mistress, he recalls, with a pang of self-contempt, that a year before he had felt like that for another woman. That, I surmise, was not at all the kind of lover he had wanted to be. It may be that constantly he saw himself through the eyes of youth and found himself wanting. Loti, in whom some saw a conceited egotist, was less satisfied with himself than the meanest cabin-boy who ever served under him.

What does Juliette Adam say of him?

"I was truly his mother, and she, the true, the gentle, used to say, 'He belongs to both of us.' And he could well belong to both, for he possessed an inexhaustible store of tenderness. Loti, who was looked on as an egotist, had in friendship, in all his relations with the rest of the world, but one thought —to give out what he had received from his visions.

"I called him 'the public solicitor'—for he never wearied of soliciting favours for others. His warmth of heart, his charity, his defence of the little and the weak, bound him in life to others. His was the most compassionate heart I ever knew."

The most compassionate. Therein lay the greatness of this man whom France rightly honours among her most brilliant men of letters. Loti wrote out of the fullness of his heart. He had no need to wear high heels—measured by his sympathy, Pierre Loti towered above the sons of men.

THE END

A SHORT BIBLIOGRAPHY

OF

THE WORKS OF PIERRE LOTI

AZIYADÉ (Stamboul, 1876-1877), Calmann-Lévy, Paris, January, 1879 (Anonymous).

LE MARIAGE DE LOTI. Calmann-Lévy, Paris, March, 1880.

LE ROMAN D'UN SPAHI. Calmann-Lévy, Paris, September, 1881.

FLEURS D'ENNUI. Calmann-Lévy, Paris, November, 1882.

MON FRÈRE YVES. Calmann-Lévy, Paris, October, 1883.

LES TROIS DAMES DE LA KASBAH. 1884.

PÊCHEUR D'ISLANDE. Calmann-Lévy, Paris, June, 1886.

PROPOS D'EXIL. Calmann-Lévy, Paris, June, 1887.

MADAME CHRYSANTHÈME. Calmann-Lévy, Paris, March, 1887.

JAPONERIES D'AUTOMNE. Calmann-Lévy, Paris, March, 1889.

AU MAROC. Calmann-Lévy, Paris, January, 1890.

LE ROMAN D'UN ENFANT. Calmann-Lévy, Paris, May, 1890.

LE LIVRE DE LA PITIÉ ET DE LA MORT. Calmann-Lévy, Paris, July, 1890.

FANTOME D'ORIENT. Calmann-Lévy, Paris, February, 1892.

UNE EXILÉE. Calmann-Lévy, Paris, May, 1893.

MATELOT. Alphonse Lemerre, Paris, 1893.

LE DÉSERT. Calmann-Lévy, January, 1895.

JÉRUSALEM. Calmann-Lévy, 1895.

LA GALILÉE. Calmann-Lévy, Paris, 1895.

RAMUNTCHO. Calmann-Lévy, 1897.

FIGURES ET CHOSES QUI PASSAIENT. Calmann-Lévy, Paris, 1898.

JUDITH RENAUDIN. 1898.

REFLETS SUR LA SOMBRE ROUTE. Calmann-Lévy, Paris, 1899.

LES DERNIERS JOURS DE PÉKIN. Calmann-Lévy, 1902.

L'INDE (SANS LES ANGLAIS). Calmann-Lévy, Paris, 1903.

VERS ISPAHAN. Calmann-Lévy, Paris, March, 1904.

LA TROISIÈME JEUNESSE DE MADAME PRUNE. Calmann-Lévy, Paris, 1905.

LES DÉSENCHANTÉES. Calmann-Lévy, Paris, 1906.

LA MORT DE PHILÆ. Calmann-Lévy, Paris, 1909.

LE CHATEAU DE LA BELLE-AU-BOIS-DORMANT. Calmann-Lévy, Paris, 1910.

UN PÈLERIN D'ANGKOR. Calmann-Lévy, Paris, 1912.

LA TURQUIE AGONISANTE. Calmann-Lévy, Paris, 1913.

LA HYÈNE ENRAGÉE. Calmann-Lévy, Paris, 1916.

QUELQUES ASPECTS DU VERTIGE MONDIAL. Flammarion, Paris, 1917.

L'HORREUR ALLEMANDE. Calmann-Lévy, Paris, 1918.

PRIME JEUNESSE. Calmann-Lévy, Paris, 1919

LA MORT DE NOTRE CHÈRE FRANCE EN ORIENT. Calmann-Lévy, Paris, 1920.

SUPRÊMES VISIONS D'ORIENT. Calmann-Lévy, Paris, 1921.

UN JEUNE OFFICIER PAUVRE. Calmann-Lévy, Paris, 1923.

TRANSLATIONS INTO ENGLISH OF THE WORKS OF PIERRE LOTI

All published by T. Werner Laurie Ltd., London, and
Frederick A. Stokes Co., New York.

INDEX